"...democracy seems to be falling apart and losing its meaning in the very countries where it has been long established and most profoundly rooted."

—Revel, *Democracy against itself (1993)*

"The new rules of globalisation—and the players writing them—focus on integrating global markets, neglecting the needs of peoples that markets cannot meet. The process is concentrating power and marginalising the poor, both countries and people."

—UN *Human development report (1999)*

"Radio and television combine technology-based change with a long history of cultural tradition, and it is precisely this encounter between the very newest and very oldest that makes the audio-visual mass media a unique meeting point in the emerging information society."

—Wessberg, in: *UNESCO's Communication and information report, 1999–2000 (1999)*

"America is currently engaged in a bold experiment to bring democracy to the Middle East. As it does so, it needs to pay a little more attention to tending the flame of democracy back home."

—*The Economist (2003)*

Tending the Flame of Democracy

Tending the Flame of Democracy

◆

A personal view by international communications expert

Geoffrey Whitehead

iUniverse, Inc.
New York Lincoln Shanghai

Tending the Flame of Democracy
A personal view by international communications expert

iUniverse, Inc.

For information address:
iUniverse, Inc.
2021 Pine Lake Road, Suite 100
Lincoln, NE 68512
www.iuniverse.com

ISBN: 0-595-30285-8

Printed in the United States of America

To my wife, Faith Barber

Contents

Acknowledgements

It was possible to compile this book only with the active support of people in many countries and having three areas of expertise: broadcasters, public officials and academics. Thank you, all. Any remaining errors and, of course, all interpretations, are my responsibility.

Introduction: Why reform must start now

This book looks at ways in which democratic institutions in the U.S.-led West could be strengthened to meet the threats of global terrorism and other challenges in the first quarter of the 21st century. It suggests that policy frameworks and institutions already exist at the international, regional and national levels. These could be used now as models to help bring about a re-gearing of policies in the interests of both the West and, perhaps ultimately, of the world as a whole—if the political will power is strong enough.

Since the bombing attacks on America on 11 September, 2001, (now known almost universally by the U.S. dating style as "9/11"), it's become clearer than ever that foreign policy begins at home. The West therefore first needs to make sure its own house is in order so that it can become a more convincing advocate of democratic processes to others. That in turn means making bigger efforts to restore faith in democratic institutions at home, with the goal of turning round the massive abstention rate in recent U.S. and British elections.

It's paradoxical that, just when the West's relative *external* power and influence is increasingly being challenged at a regional and global level by both states and non-government organisation—some just plain terrorist factions—from other civilisations, research is also showing more public dissatisfaction than before with democratic institutions *within* the older Western democracies.

So the book's also about the debilitating impacts on democracy inherited by today's Western political leaders from their predecessors, especially those who held power in the last quarter of the 20th century. This state of affairs flows directly from the coincidental arrival in that period of the information communications technology (ICT) revolution, and the widespread adoption of the global free market ideology by governments of the political left as well as of the right. Perhaps even more importantly, it also stems from the way in which policies to exploit that accidental synergy were decided and implemented.

A number of critics of globalisation attack multi-national companies themselves for the growing imbalance in our lives in today's world. Others recognise that it was, in fact, the governing elites—often, just a handful of politicians and like-minded officials—who took the extreme political and economic free market and de-regulation decisions in the 1980s and 1990s, which allowed that imbalance to come about.

Although those decisions were taken by democratically elected governments, they often did not fully consult, or even adequately inform, their people about the strategic choices they were making at the time. Nor did they draw attention to the probable longer term democratic, social and cultural implications of such policies. In some instances the consequences were not foreseen by the decision makers themselves; in others, they were foreseen but not explored by policy advisers as fully as they might have been. In some cases they were not explored at all.

There's little doubt that two of the major challenges now facing the West, the external challenge from people having different cultural values, interpreted by some in extreme forms and backed by force, and the internal challenge of public apathy towards established democratic processes, will gather importance in the upcoming quarter century. It will therefore be an extremely significant transitional period in terms of both domestic policies and of international relations, and of the necessary interplay between them.

It is, clearly, both in the domestic political self-interest and the external national self-interest of Western governments to face up to the policy gaps of the recent past and to develop, as a matter of urgent priority, a new range of integrated public policies that will be more relevant to our citizenship needs in the first quarter of the 21st century. This must include a recognition that 'the market' has failed to meet all our communications needs and that there is, therefore, an important role for the state in that particular activity.

I think that role is justified more than ever before because this will also be a transitional quarter century for people in terms of their ability to access and use new forms of communications. While, for example, 500 million people worldwide were estimated to have access to the Internet in 2001, there was no publicity to the other side of the equation: that 5,500 million people didn't have such access, and that many of them would never even make a telephone call in their lives. So people will come to terms with the new technologies, if at all, at different rates. Many will continue to rely on print, radio and television as their primary sources of information, complemented for some, but not replaced, by the new technologies.

In an increasingly globalised world this situation creates a third, additional major challenge for Western governments and their policy advisers, especially for the U.S., which currently holds a comparative advantage in the era of global information, as in many other things.

As former top U.S. defence and intelligence official Joseph S. Nye (now dean of the Kennedy School of Government at Harvard) has argued, "the market will not suffice" if foreign policy objectives are to be achieved. Nor will it suffice to meet domestic policy challenges, or the challenge of differing rates of acceptance of change. That's why I think it's important for the U.S. and other Western governments to re-examine now, and urgently, whether, why and how the state should intervene in the information communications market place.

One important tool is already in place in most Western states through the public stake in internal and external communications, where it still exists. Where they do have strong, established public service multi-media programme content providers like Britain's BBC, Canada's CBC and Australia's ABC, their legislative terms of reference need to be reviewed. Sadly, and importantly, the U.S. never has had a strong equivalent and so its needs for a policy re-appraisal are even more dire.

In all cases, though, Western governments need to re-assess how new policy objectives for these programme providers could help their citizens have a better understanding of the need for Nye's "vertical connections" between domestic and foreign policies in this new "post-9/11" era. If, as I believe, such re-appraisals find that unbalanced market forces have driven the public sector too far into the swamp of unwinnable ratings wars as entertainment vehicles, then I think the old mantra of 'inform and educate' should be put back at the top of the agenda, and 'entertain' set as a secondary objective, to showcase emerging local talent.

◆   ◆   ◆

So more people need to take on board the fact that it's primarily governments and their advisers, and not the usual targets, the trans-national corporations, that hold the heavy responsibility for the consequences of the neglect of key aspects of public policy development in the last quarter of the 20th century. These policy gaps have left important democratic and other institutions weakened and marginalised in ways that could have been avoided, but can now be put right relatively easily.

My focus, therefore, is not so much on the success or failure of the market itself as on the responsibilities of elected governments and their policy advisers for past decisions or past inertia. They do, of course, have a continuing power to decide or influence events in ways more beneficial to Western democracy in particular, and possibly to global human development in general, in the immediate future.

I believe there's a pivotal role to be played by public service broadcasters re-defined as public sector multi-media programme providers: to provide a better balance in a communications world in which 'demo' has come, for too long and to our overall loss, to mean 'demographics' rather than 'democracy:' a world of tabloid media communications.

◆   ◆   ◆

This book is aimed at stimulating interest and debate among the general public which has, by and large, been excluded from effective input to strategic policy choices in the last quarter of the 20th century. It will also be of interest to students who want to look at communications studies through the unfamiliar lens of international political culture. For those who want to undertake further research, or whose task it is to develop policy choices for today's governments, I've provided a substantial selection of source material and primary data in a series of Appendixes, which was harder to put together than you might think. Many of these references have been drawn from the last decade or so, and therefore have a continuing relevance to our new world.

The period between now and 2025 is going to be a transitional quarter century like no other.

December 2003.

1

The triple challenges to democracy

The West: selling itself short

When President George W. Bush of the United States finally took office on 20 January, 2001, the mass of briefing papers prepared for him should have included an holistic overview of policy options looking as far ahead as the year 2025. First, acknowledging that foreign policy *does* begin at home, then taking a 'helicopter' view of the interplay between key domestic and key external policies and suggesting future integrated policy choices.

I hope they did, and that they also included a realistic assessment of the current status, and possible future development, of U.S. communications policies in this global context, both from the international, public, interests of the West as a whole as well as from the national, predominantly private, interests of the U.S. itself.

This is because I believe that the West, and especially the U.S., has so far sold itself short in preparing for the global debate in the 21st century about values and ideals between people of different civilisations, cultures and histories. Its preoccupation with free market economic ideology has left other public policy choices often ignored, marginalised and un-debated.

It simply doesn't make sense for this state of affairs to continue if we are to get through the first quarter of the 21st century in better shape than we did in the last quarter of the 20th century.

The monologue of the market has to come to an end and be replaced by a structured dialogue between the state and its citizens in the wider context of different needs and different policy choices in an increasingly globalised world. This has to come about as a result of conscious and collective decisions by governments in the West. Otherwise it just won't happen.

1

The best and potentially the most efficient facilitator for that debate will be a state-funded, free-to-all, nationwide multi-media programme provider, formally recognised as an important democratic institution in its own right. It should have a statutory right of distribution, using all the most relevant and cost-effective new technologies as they become available as well as the traditional communications vehicles of television, radio and print.

Its remit, or terms of reference, should be to give all people the *opportunity* to gain a common knowledge of policy options facing their country's leaders so that they have a better chance to understand and influence those choices and, who knows, even to help governments achieve better outcomes.

With the glaring exception of the U.S., which doesn't have such an effective national body as a result of past policy decisions, most Western states already have such a programme provider—their public service broadcasters, many of them now around eighty years old. They are not dinosaurs, but precious assets awaiting a rebirth.

The contract between the state and these broadcasters, explicit, through legislation, or through other forms of written understanding like the BBC's agreement with the government of the day, now needs urgent re-appraisal throughout the West. This is because of the triple challenges facing democracies: external shifts in relative power structures; internal apathy towards domestic democratic institutions; and the wide gap between early and late starters, and between heavy and light users, of information communications technologies (ICTs), what's now being called the "digital divide."

The amount of policy change needed in these contracts will turn, in part, on the rate of movement by governments towards 'economic freedom' in the past twenty years and the degree of protection and development given to these public institutions in the same period. For some, the only answer will be a need for completely new communications institutions; for others, radical reform or, in some cases, fine tuning of existing ones.

And because the strategies of the dozen or so multi-media "world companies" now fragmenting domestic markets are on a world scale, policy thinking about the revised role for the public sector in communications—what the Canadians notably called "a public lane on the information highway"—needs to begin at the global level of analysis, too.

The global challenge: "Who are we?"

Starting from that wider context, public communications policies should reaffirm where each country fits in at the civilisational level. Then they should acknowledge the role of the state towards its people as citizens, not as consumers, in this new, globalised, free market world. Finally, they need to re-examine the wants and needs of indigenous peoples, or of varying ethnic groups and nations within a state, against that matrix. That is the new agenda, replacing the private v. public sector debate of the 1980s and 1990s, or such debate as was then allowed.

The American political scientist, Samuel P. Huntington, is one of a group of 20th century writers who has identified half a dozen remaining civilisations in the world: the Sinic, Japanese, Hindu, Islamic, Orthodox Russian and Western. They each, he argues, have different values which, if ignored, can lead to friction *between* civilisations but which, if acknowledged, can also bring states *within* each civilisation closer.

And within the West, he's identified an Anglo-Saxon core linking Britain, the U.S., Canada, Australia and New Zealand. Because I've worked at a senior level for public service broadcasters in three of those countries, that core, plus Celtic Ireland, to offer another small-state example, is the focus of this book.

The pivotal question for the 21st century that all states must answer, says Huntington, is, "Who are we?"

This will become an increasingly critical issue as states from "the rest," in his terms, make it more explicit that they want a greater say in how their own region, and the world, is governed in the new century. The composition of the institutions set up by the West at the end of the Second World War in 1945, and maybe the institutions themselves, will look very different in 2025 and even more so as the decades roll by.

The U.S., Britain and France and their allies, including Canada, Australia and New Zealand, the Western democratic victors over totalitarianism as represented by Hitler's Germany, Mussolini's Italy and Hirohito's Japan, will no longer be ruling the roost to the same extent as power relativities change. China, Japan, India, the Islamic states and a "new" Russia will all want to see a more multi-polar world. By late 2003, for example, Germany, a war-time loser, began hinting that it would now like a permanent seat on the U.N. Security Council.

It's easy for the generations now in power in the West to forget that the outcome of the conflict between democracy and totalitarianism was touch-and-go in the early 1940s, and that the global ascendancy of the Western democratic form of government is a relatively recent event. It was only in the last few years of the

20th century, following the end of the East-West "Cold War" in the period 1989–91, that U.S. President Clinton was able to claim that for the first time in history a majority of the world's six billion people were being governed by democracies.

But the 21st century West will doubtless continue to advocate political and civil rights to the rest of the world, especially its own democratic forms of government and their accompanying human rights, even though people from these other civilisations, notably China, might not necessarily see democracy as their ultimate political destination. They, like much of the rest of the world, are in any event currently giving higher priorities to economic than to social reforms.

The problem for the West in this global debate about differing objectives and priorities is that it has an Achilles heel that has been evident to its own citizens for some time, and which, unless the right sort of corrective action is taken, and soon, will be increasingly evident to the international recipients of its missionary zeal, too.

The domestic challenge: "Can vote—won't vote"

The great paradox is this: just as more of the world's people are coming to live under the banner of democracy, citizens within the established Western democracies—the advocates—are becoming increasingly critical of the relevance and effectiveness of their own civic institutions and so increasingly apathetic about the wider democratic process.

In the U.S., for example, a Harris poll alienation index that had averaged twenty-nine in the 1960s rose six points, from fifty-six to sixty-two, during 1999 for a 1990s average of sixty-three. Values studies elsewhere in the West reflected similar trends.

This broad trend is partly a result of some Western governments maintaining a relatively closed system of decision-making, especially during the last fifteen to twenty years of transition towards "more market" policies. At the same time, some have adopted the strategy of denigrating the past in order to make the present seem more palatable to older generations and to seem more successful than in some ways it undoubtedly is to its younger admirers, "the children of the free market."

This more absolute and overt determination to control both the agenda and the scope of debate on key new domestic strategies became widespread at almost the exact moment (about 1985) when, at the international level, both the communist world and Third World states began to turn away from their historically closed systems and looked to at least a form of democracy as the key to their future economic salvation. With it they accepted a need to open up public information and debate that had been closed, in Russia's case, for some seventy-five years. Their citizens have responded enthusiastically to these new-found freedoms, although they're still working through their new-found responsibilities.

Within the West, the opposite shift, towards a tighter control of debate by shortening, or side-stepping altogether, democratic processes, and by using public relations consultants—the "spin doctors"—as never before to put a favourable gloss on events, is adding to the wider disillusionment of many of its citizens. Better-educated electorates recognised the drift towards an autocratic style of government within their democracies, even though they may not have fully understood at first how it happened, or how best to articulate their concerns. That is now changing.

This disenchantment with politicians and their institutions is reflected more often than not in low turnouts for elections in those countries where voting isn't compulsory (unlike Australia, where it is). It was perhaps one of the ultimate ironies of the 20th century that President Clinton was re-elected in 1996 by only about forty-seven million votes out of a total electoral roll of some 193 million. Of the balance, another forty-seven million voted for other candidates, while the rest simply stayed at home. So overall, President Clinton's mandate came from only some twenty-four percent of the electorate. The forty-nine percent turnout of voters was the lowest since 1932. The comparable turnout figure in the cliff-hanger 2000 election of President George W. Bush wasn't much better at just 51.3 percent.

In Britain, the 71.5 percent turnout in its 1997 general election, though relatively high compared with the U.S., was nevertheless the lowest there since 1935. By late 2000 opinion polls were showing that forty-nine percent of Britons thought their country was becoming less democratic under Tony Blair's Labour government which, after all, had its historical roots in the principles of social democracy. By the 2001 general election turnout had dropped again, to an abysmal 59.4 percent, the lowest turnout since 1918.

The outcome of the Cold War was seen as an almost inevitable victory for the West by its post-Second World War generation of ruling elites, rather than as a consequence of an internal crumbling of the Soviet form of communism, which it largely was. This is perhaps one reason why they've seen no obvious need or priority to strengthen and re-vitalise democratic processes at home. For them it's the winning system, and the rest of the world would benefit by going along with it.

But that isn't necessarily so. The French writer, Jean-Francois Revel, for instance, believes that "democracy remains, at best, a possible outcome of a drawn-out fight for power."

I think history's on his side.

The communications challenge: "change and continuity"

When historians of the late 21st century come to write their retrospective analyses of the information communications technology (ICT) revolution—the third revolution, following those in agriculture and industry—they'll find that it had no clear beginning in global terms and no definite end. In fact, it will almost certainly still be in progress. They'll also find that it won't fit neatly into the artificial divisions of years, decades and centuries; and they'll almost certainly conclude that for most people it was in reality more of an evolution than a revolution.

This evolution certainly began in the early 1980s when the now famous "accidental synergy" happened. This was the coincidental development of technology, allowing direct broadcast by satellite into peoples' homes—homes increasingly equipped with personal computers giving access to the Internet and e-mail—and the sudden dominance within leading Western states of free market economic policies: President Reagan's era in the United States and the Margaret Thatcher years in Britain. Other Western states were caught up in the same tide, though to differing degrees and so with varying social, cultural and, I think most importantly, differing democratic consequences.

The global application of all this was undoubtedly given a push by the unexpected ending of the Cold War. This, for example, allowed the U.S. to release the Internet, which had originally been developed within the U.S. for defence purposes, on an unsuspecting world as recently as 1995. Within five years its early promise of being primarily an engine for academic research and the free exchange of ideas had, however, been tainted by its increasing use for pornography and the electronic equivalent of hate mail. It was increasingly, too, just another vehicle for commercialisation.

And so within the fifteen or so years between, say, 1985 and 2000, the first phase of the revolution/evolution had taken off. But it's easy for early and high users of the new range of technologies to forget that this new world applies only to some. At the millennium, more than half the world's population still didn't own a telephone and would never make a telephone call in their lives. More than sixty percent of telephone lines in 1996 were in twenty-three countries representing only fifteen percent of the world's people. So the new ICT world was still largely a tool for those with both access and the ability to pay for it: governments, commerce and academic institutions, rather than for a majority of households, even in the West.

All this, of course, was changing relatively quickly, with the Internet gaining new subscribers worldwide daily. Nevertheless, UN Educational, Social and Cultural Organisation (UNESCO) estimates of connections by 1998 were of just between fifty and eighty million people, and with only between a hundred and two hundred million people estimated for 2002. The numbers of people worldwide estimated to be on-line in 1999 was a hundred and fifty-eight million, with a huge imbalance in favour of industrial countries like the U.S., Japan and the European Union (EU), where eighty-five percent of the world's Internet hosts were jointly to be found, over developing countries. There was an equally startling gender imbalance in favour of male users.

Even if these estimates are out by a hundred percent, the resulting total is still only a fraction of the global population of six billion. The information Utopia certainly hadn't arrived for all by the start of the 21st century, despite the enthusiasm of early starters reinforced by the marketing hype of telecoms and related businesses seeking to identify and expand global opportunities as fast as possible.

Television, radio and print not only remained the primary systems of communications for most people, but I think are likely to stay so for at least another twenty-five years until the technological potentials for a convergence of services and simpler delivery systems (the PC v the TV battle) have been sorted out, and price levels become affordable by the majority.

As Arne Wessberg, chief executive of the Finnish Broadcasting Company, one of those quoted at the front of this book, has pointed out, enthusiasm for potential opportunities opened up by new technologies "often leads to an over-estimation of the significance and pace of change in the mass media." I agree. Most people, as he says, want and need a degree of continuity in their lives. They favour constancy and permanence, and so policy planning should both build this continuity factor into account and give it equal weight when making assumptions about an achievable and acceptable rate of change.

The rate of change can be over-estimated as well as under-estimated. A television programme screened in late 1999 recalled the forecasts of ten-year-olds in 1975 of what life would be like in 2000. Most of them expected far greater and more fundamental changes than actually happened. Now that this generation is able to make or influence policy decisions, I think it's at least possible that it might make the same mistake about the period from now to 2025.

Policy leaders and policy laggards

In the new era of the information revolution, practice has a long way to go before it matches promise. That's why I think more serious thought needs to be given by policy-makers to the development of policy options recognising the sense of grafting new systems on to established content providers, like the public service broadcasters, where it hasn't happened already. They then need to recognise the probability of an ICT evolution rather than a revolution. Finally, they need to provide adequate levels of public funding to allow these redefined public services to be delivered without impairing the quality of traditional services.

In particular, governments of the high-tech leadership states of the West mustn't be allowed to hide behind the soft option of pretending that they can abandon their responsibilities to their citizens in this quarter century on the grounds that their needs can now be met by the market and its new technologies, because they won't.

The state has to intervene if a better balance is to be restored to our lives. After all, as U.S. lawyer and analyst, Monroe E. Price, puts it, "there is no national identity of Murdoch, no flag or loyalty to Disney." Of course not. But some free market Western governments have been behaving as if the market *can* meet all our needs when it's not its job to do so. Its task is to provide entertainment and yield audience "tonnage" for global advertisers and profits for its owners while meeting our wants as consumers. It does all these things very well.

In the last fifteen years there's been a much sharper focus by private sector policy-makers in the handful of giant transnational multi-media firms, the "world companies." They've been the policy leaders: much clearer about their objectives, and much more determined to achieve their goals. One of their major achievements has been to persuade governments to switch the focus of global communications policies from the ideals and values of free speech and human rights to the market-driven realities of the World Trade Organisation (WTO).

Television is, any case, primarily an entertainment medium. As such, it's been labelled by Andrew Heyward, news president of one of the dominant North American networks, Columbia Broadcasting System (CBS), as having seven deadly sins: "imitation, predictability, artificiality, laziness, over-simplification, hype and cynicism." Now, the increasing fragmentation of broadcast communications markets and the intensified battle for market share to justify on-going financing has led many public service broadcasters to join in the further dumbing-down of television programming and scheduling.

Most significantly, the content and style of its news bulletins have in some instances been trivialised just when the public needs facts, contexts and credible analysis as never before if they are to work their way through what the BBC has called "the information maze" of the 21st century.

Instead, some public sector television channels have responded to the new market challenge by adopting U.S.-style news bulletins. These now have an emphasis on crime coverage; entertainment promos dressed up as news stories; choreographed chit-chat between news anchors in peak time, always an avuncular man with a pretty woman, often a generation younger. They end with a "soft" item, preferably the obligatory pet stories favoured by advertisers so that the news audience is in a more receptive mood for the next commercial break.

Governments, meanwhile, have either taken a conscious decision to pull the state out of the market in the optimistic or naïve belief that the market will provide, or let these policy choices go by default, which is just as bad. It's the job of the state to meet our needs as citizens. But politicians and the public alike have long taken for granted, and so ignored, the role of public service broadcasters as democratic institutions in their own right. This role is, therefore, currently being undermined, not by ideological opponents or by market forces, but as a direct result of public policy neglect.

There's been a failure in many Western countries to think afresh soon enough, and in sufficiently radical terms, about the changing role of the state in communications in this increasingly globalised world. In some cases there's been a lack of political willpower to implement to the full even those relatively limited changes suggested to them.

Because of these failures in public policy the relative balances of the recent past, never perfect, are now tipping strongly in favour of this new, globalised, private sector. The marketplace has become asymmetrical.

Political decisions led to the dual process of the economic shift to the "new right" by governments of both the left and the right and to the introduction of deregulated, or very lightly regulated, communications markets, allowing these new players to maximise their opportunities. But it's very debatable whether the primary "driver" of both forces, the United States, foresaw all the consequences of the interplay between the two, especially on the nature of democracy in the West.

But by acts of commission or of omission, governments *did* allow this situation to develop, and so they must also provide new answers to our changing 21st century needs.

Unless corrective action is taken soon, the West may become vulnerable to charges from its critics that its human rights and democratic records at home are not as good as they might be. If that perception becomes widespread, its ability to influence others successfully in the upcoming change period will be impaired.

The key questions are: How are Western democratic governments going to manage change in the communications industry in the immediate future? And will the public policy decisions they take help reinvigorate their forms of democracy, so that we are better able to cope with the interplay between the three major challenges facing us all by the world of 2025?

2

Meeting the challenges: communications for citizenship

The market can, and does, fail

Western governments need to take the threshold decisions that there *is* such a thing as market failure, that this is now very clear in the broadcast communications industry and that there *is* a case for effective state intervention in that market.

Politicians and their policy advisers alike need to look at the issue from the starting point of what's been called "communications for citizenship."

The perennial question put by treasury officials worldwide is: "Should the state be involved in this activity at all, and if so, at what minimum cost?" But this needs to be balanced by a question put from the democratic and human rights perspective: "How can the state *not* afford to be involved in this activity, and what is the best range of services possible that can be publicly financed within overall budget parameters?"

Once this political question has been resolved, the economic case for state intervention in the market can be justified using the "merit good" argument. This is used more often to justify the provision of other public services like schools and hospitals. Basically, the argument is that such services have a collective benefit to the community as a whole greater than to any individual.

Advocates of increased local programme content usually rely on the national cultural identity argument, and the knock on economic benefits of more locally-made programmes stimulating an independent programme production industry. I support that cause, although officials often see it as providing a service for, perhaps, just fifteen to twenty percent of the population. This, however, often leads to public broadcasting services scoring low policy priorities and low levels of government financing. The result is, inevitably, a marginalised organisation.

11

I put the state's democratic human rights obligations to its citizens at the top of the list, because this justifies state intervention in the market-place on behalf of one hundred percent of the population.

It isn't just the *volume* of local content that matters, but the *range and quality* of its content: quotas, if set, are easily met by low-cost quiz shows and other mass-appeal, entertainment-driven, programmes mimicking those already on offer from the private sector. They end up providing the viewer with "more of the same," as all providers fight over the same under-thirty disposable income demographics.

In my view, the rationale for a public service multi-media programme provider in the 21st century is the same as that in the establishment years of the early 20th century, but with its mantra of "to inform, educate and entertain" having a sharper focus and one more relevant to our new needs.

The sequence of priorities should still be the same, though. Information, but with content and presentation designed to help everyone to have an equal *opportunity*—whether they sample it or not—to gain a common knowledge of issues, allowing them to think harder about across-the-board policy choices. Education, but in the widest possible sense, seeing human development as the ultimate justification for economic development and including, for example, advice on how to get, and keep, jobs. And entertainment, but with an obligation to showcase in prime time the work of emerging local talent, rather than competing with the multi-national private sector's "blockbusters."

In the language of governments, these are the provider outputs necessary to achieve a required political outcome: in this case, a better informed and educated citizenry.

A critical world split: programme exporters and importers

Policy makers, asked to develop new strategic options for governments to consider, need to take account of the past and recognise the effects on their people of the historical split between programme exporting countries and programme importing countries. They then need to accept that these effects are being rapidly intensified in a globalised, free market world.

This will help them to identify the degree of current democratic, cultural and social risk and, consequently, to assess the degree of potential benefits that can be achieved through corrective policy development and implementation.

In the importing countries of the "core" West I rate Canada (which imports some thirty percent of its programmes) as having a relatively low risk and enjoying relatively high democratic, social and cultural benefits because of its long, and, so far successful fight for a national identity independent from that of its neighbour, the U.S.; and because it has developed an integrated legislative framework to help achieve this. Australia (twenty percent of imports) I judge as also having a relatively low risk, but with existing benefits capable of improvement through fine tuning of policy to make some of its legislative frameworks both more relevant to the needs of the 21st century and more integrated. Ireland (sixty percent) and New Zealand (seventy-five percent) I see as vulnerable, high risk countries needing reform; in New Zealand's case, more radical reform.

The programme exporting countries need reform, too. The United States needs to re-consider its policies and structures in a broader context and perhaps invent a new public service broadcaster closer to West European models. Its Public Broadcasting Service (PBS), set up in 1969 as a private, non-profit corporation, grew from a Federal Communications Commission (FCC) report on educational broadcasting adopted in 1952 and implemented by the *Public Broadcasting Act 1967* which also has a narrow, educational, focus (Appendix 3 (a) (ii)).

Above all, political decision-makers in the West and their policy advisers mustn't be allowed by the public to get away with former British Prime Minister Margaret Thatcher's rationale for fundamental economic reform: "TINA: There Is No Alternative."

There always *are* alternatives, and I believe the Western democracies can't afford *not* to look at alternatives if they want to be in good shape by the very different world of 2025.

Programme exporters: "US/UK"

United States: the "business" model

The historical U.S. approach to broadcasting and the way it reflects its society has always been radically different from the West European concept, which is based on values. In the U.S. broadcasting is and always has been primarily a business.

There's never been any political will to establish a powerful, nationwide public service broadcaster like Britain's BBC. This is partly because the Constitution, and the 1791 First Amendment to it, put down markers to limit potential government influence on the principle of free speech (Appendix 3 (a) (i)). But it's also to do with a combination of political and business self-interests in what is essentially a conservative country.

To an outside observer it seems astonishing that the practical application to communications policies of this 18th century statement of ideals hasn't been rigorously and effectively re-examined in the light of late 20th and early 21st century communications needs. One North American analyst has labelled this as "the debate that was never undertaken," while another has described the outcome as "a fundamental error which has caused grave cultural deprivation not only in the U.S. but also to all the world."

That's my point, too. In a world in which the influence of a state is increasingly considered to be as important, if not more important, than power itself, it seems perverse that the U,S, is selling itself and its Western partners short by letting the world see its society through the single lens of mass-appeal entertainment when it has far more to offer.

Yet that's been the inevitable outcome of the combination of political and business decisions dating back to 1934 when the Federal Communications Commission was set up as a regulatory body to allocate frequencies, grant licenses, limit foreign ownership and so on, but with no authority over programme content.

But the ever-expanding domestic market of cable and satellite television, which began in the U.S. with the advent of the Telstar satellite in the early 1960s, hasn't led to a greater range of programme choice (more doesn't necessarily mean better) or to a widespread distribution, in peak time, of quality programming. The U.S. domestic market system has failed to establish a tradition of such nationwide programming to meet the needs of people as better informed citizens and so, perhaps, to encourage them to be more positive about taking part in the democratic process by voting at election times. Continuing low voter turnouts are evidence of this. Democracy needs reinvigorating in the U.S. just as much as anywhere else, and an effective, nationwide, public system of human communications should be part of the deal.

The result of this policy neglect has been a major imbalance of viewer choice, leading to regular calls for government intervention to redress the imbalance. But successive governments have so far been at best neutral towards the concept of a stronger system of public service broadcasting, or a new institutional model more relevant to 21st century needs, despite these repeated pressures for change.

Price, the U.S. lawyer and analyst, says the decentralised, marginalising model for public television was developed because the Nixon administration of the 1970s didn't want a strong central entity that might help nourish a strong public, on the grounds that public broadcasting was in the hands of "forces creating allegiances hostile to more conservative values."

But it's ironical, to say the least, that it was this model of broadcasting that the U.S. promoted to the transitional democracies of the former Soviet Union and the Third World emerging after the Cold War in the last decade of the 20th century. It's a model out of balance. As a business, marketing products first within the U.S. and now also as a vehicle for expanding U.S. trade within the global market, it does very well in meeting our needs as consumers. But many of its own people consider that it falls short of meeting their own needs (let alone anyone else's) as citizens.

Britain: the "values" model

In complete contrast with the U.S. model, broadcasting in Britain, as in many other West European countries, began as a values-driven public service monopoly. Partly because of an initial scarcity of frequencies, it was based on networks broadcasting nationwide. This monopoly lasted for about thirty years and so became the norm against which other developments were judged at the time.

The second phase began in the mid-1950s, when Conservative governments allowed privately-owned commercial television companies into the market. Locally-based commercial radio stations came later still, long behind their North American counterparts. Both industries were, however, relatively highly regulated for several decades compared with the more recent free market era of the 1980s and 1990s.

The second half-century therefore began with the BBC, Britain's original public service broadcaster, actively engaging in an evolution of the market into what became known as a "comfortable duopoly" between two BBC television channels, the more popular BBC-1 and the more demanding BBC-2, sharing the audience, more or less on a fifty-fifty basis overall, with two private sector channels. These were Independent Television (ITV), originally a mosaic of regionally-based companies; and, since 1980, a minority taste Channel 4. This was to be increasingly recognised as falling within the public service ethic in its own right, despite its reliance on commercial revenues.

This was still a relatively cohesive market, with the predominance of nationwide networking echoing Britain's then unitary form of government (pre-devolution to Scotland and Wales at the end of the century) and one also widely seen as reinforcing social cohesion. What had undoubtedly been a bias towards "high culture" programming in the BBC's earlier days had certainly come to an end with Sir Hugh Greene's era as a populist director-general in the 1960s, and that mirrored the social and cultural changes of the time.

Within the duopoly market, which lasted from the mid-1950s to the late 1980s, the BBC became highly skilled at achieving, and then maintaining, both a populist and a complementary, more demanding, approach to public sector broadcasting, each within the values ethic. That is what it exported to the world too, though with a transatlantic content increasingly evident as British producers broadened their market base to embrace more U.S. co-productions.

Enter Rupert Murdoch

Everything changed with the third era of television, the far more fragmented markets stemming from the entry of multi-channel services owned by world companies like Rupert Murdoch's News Corp, which began in earnest in Britain with the arrival of his BSkyB in 1989 and soon cut into the market share of both BBC-1 and the earlier ITV companies.

Nobody, in my view, can go down market as skilfully as the BBC if it sees its audience base, and therefore a major justification for its financing levels, at risk. The ITV companies, the new status quo, fought back in the same way. So it was ironic that it was in the fundamentalist free market political eras of Margaret Thatcher and John Major, when conservative family values were at the top of the political agenda, that the deregulated communications system they had brought about unleashed on British audiences programmes featuring sexuality, violence and coarse language as never before.

This overall down-market response to the increasing fragmentation of Britain's newly-competitive domestic television market was then also exported to the world. Inevitably, this magnified the effect of a bias towards more tabloid television already emerging within programme-importing countries as an inevitable consequence of the widespread espousal by their own governments of free market ideologies and communications systems.

But by 1999, BBC-1's share of the viewing audience had dropped below thirty percent for the first time ever and Channel 4 was occasionally out-rating BBC-2 as well. Some experts forecast further problems for both the BBC and the original ITV commercial companies in the early years of the 21st century as the new private operators built up from their earlier audience bases.

This BBC strategy of fighting the new competition on its own mass-appeal, commercial ratings-driven ground came increasingly into question as the 20th century ended. After a House of Lords debate critical of some aspects of the

BBC's programming direction the corporation's governors declared that the BBC mustn't be ruled by ratings but remain "unashamedly public service" and "dare to be different." Their then newly-appointed director-general, Greg Dyke, declared his determination in 1999 to put educational programming into the front line, seeing this as "the most critical lever in shaping the prosperity and stability of individuals, companies, and the UK as a whole."

That's also part of my argument for seeing public service television in a human rights/human development context.

But today's BBC managers are facing the challenges of a much more fragmented and competitive market than ever before. In differing degrees, this has been the lot addressed by public broadcasters in Canada, Australia, and elsewhere in the West for many years and with varying degrees of success. In those days, some senior BBC executives were rather patronising about the relatively lower market share then being achieved by their international colleagues. I don't think the current generation of BBC managers would take that stance now that they're in the same boat!

All public service broadcasters now face the same new and more intense challenges, stemming from the combined effects of globalisation, free market de-regulation, and the spread of satellite, cable and PC-based technologies.

How the governments of the majority, programme-importing countries, respond in policy terms to the new situation depends on the political and public perception of the need for state intervention to provide more effective and relevant balances to the institutionalised, entertainment-driven, exports of the U.S. and to the market-distorted exports of the last decade or so from Britain.

Programme importers: Canada and Australia: holding the line?

Canada: "the state or the United States"

There are many parallels between Canada and Australia, most obviously, of course, their size and the accompanying "tyranny of distance" problems; but there are some important distinctions, too. One of these is that constitutionally, Canada is one of the loosest confederations in the world, apart from Switzerland; while Australia has a federal constitution with relatively stronger central political powers and responsibilities. Another, of course, is that Canada has always had to fight harder to keep its identity separate from that of the U.S., its bigger and brasher neighbour to the south. Australia, both a continent and an enormous island stretching from the Pacific to the Indian oceans, has been able to exercise more choice (a choice, though, to embrace U.S. culture to a large degree, and voluntarily too, especially since the Pacific fighting alliances of the Second World War).

For Canada though, its different cultural heritage starting point is best summarised as: "the state or the United States"—one of the slogans of the Canadian Radio League in the debates before the first Canadian Broadcasting Act, setting up what is now the Canadian Broadcasting Corporation (CBC), Canada's original public service broadcaster, in 1932. Together with Canada's trans-continental railway, the CBC was seen from the start as an essential tool in state-building, and despite occasional political suggestions for its partial privatisation, it remains so for many people today.

· Its origins, like those of the world's other public broadcasting models, came about in the radio era, and its legislation was a political acknowledgement of the potential and actual cultural, political and economic impacts of what was then a relatively new medium. It was a pressing issue then because the majority of Canada's people (now thirty million) live within two hundred miles of the long border with the United States. It became an even more pressing issue in the second half of the 20th century, with the dominance of television as a medium, with its multiple cross-border distribution systems of terrestrial signals, cable and satellite.

Canadians have long been exposed to U.S. broadcasting signals, and nearly all commercial ones as well, reinforcing the south-north marketing pull across the borders of a state which itself lies along an east-west axis. In effect, the Canadian experience has been a dress rehearsal for the world's current needs, because "Americanisation" was almost synonymous with "globalisation" in its early stages.

Others can therefore learn from Canada's decision to set out in legislation the concept that Canadian broadcasting is a single system, owned and controlled by Canadians, and that *all* providers have an obligation to operate as a public service "essential to the maintenance and enhancement of national identity and cultural sovereignty" (Appendix: 3 (c) (i)).

As part of the implementation of this political intent the CBC has institutional linkages with Canadian Heritage, a government department with direct responsibility for cultural development, heritage, citizenship and Canadian identity. This mightn't have much practical effect, but I see it as an important step in terms of both the public and political perceptions of the place of public service broadcasting in machinery of government terms, if nothing else.

Unlike Britain, Canada has long had an independent regulatory authority for the system as a whole: the Canadian Radio-Television and Communications Commission (CRTC) which has been working through a programme to change the regulatory culture into a light touch system, using what it describes as "the full tool box," moving from protection through to promotion, and from judicial process towards a more collaborative process.

All this has its domestic critics. Some see a continuing gap between policy and practice, and the promise of public broadcasting "more often than not a pious wish." The outgoing chief executive of TVOntario and one of the initiators of Public Broadcasters International (PBI), Bernard Ostry, was more scathing at its opening conference in Toronto, Canada, in 1991. By developing advanced communications technologies, he argued, Canadians had effectively set themselves up for "massive foreign cultural invasions." Canada, he said, was "notorious for having devised its own cultural suicide machine..."

It is, however, hard to see how such technological change could have been avoided, and his call for a form of globalisation of public television through cooperation in the provision of services and their distribution is a goal which currently seems as far off as ever.

But on a global scale, I believe that the Canadian system is still one of the most relevant models for meeting contemporary needs within the prevailing ideological free market framework. I think Canadians work harder than most at public discussion; see more clearly than most states the linkages between content services and economic benefits, and the linkages between a Canadian identity at home and a specific Canadian presence in its external relations.

Australia: the case for fine tuning

Australia's cultural starting point in the radio era of the 1920s, like its neighbour, New Zealand's, was more to do with a maintenance of continuity of cultural identity with Britain than a concern with the U.S. This changed substantially, and finally, in favour of the U.S. following the fall of Britain's imperial outpost of Singapore to the Japanese in 1942. The consequential closer defence links across the Pacific with the U.S. soon led to an adoption, first by Australia, much later by New Zealand, of a form of cultural identity with the U.S., too.

So it isn't surprising that in the television era of the 1950s, both Antipodean countries took a hybrid approach to broadcasting, trying to achieve the best from both the British "values" and U.S. "business" models, but with the American commercial approach, especially to television broadcasting, winning out in the end.

Australia, like Canada but unlike New Zealand, at least held the line by retaining public sector broadcasting as a distinctive, non-commercial, entity. By 1980 it had not just one such television broadcaster but two as the multi-cultural Special Broadcasting Service (SBS) was expanded from its original community radio base and set up to complement more completely the traditional services of the Australian Broadcasting Corporation (ABC). Currently both Australian bodies are still operating within the "values" model.

Again like Canada, Australia's *Broadcasting Services Act 1992* (see: Appendix 3 (d) (i)) has an industry-wide remit as well as a strong focus on the private, commercial sector, covering threshold issues like cross-media ownership and local content quotas. Like the *Canadian Broadcasting Act 1991*, this has among its objectives the promotion of broadcasting services "in developing and reflecting a sense of Australian identity, character and cultural diversity." So there's an interplay between that legislation and the more specific separate legislation governing the ABC and SBS (Appendixes 3 (d) (ii) and (iv)).

By 1998 the federal government policy objectives of the SBS within this broader industry policy umbrella had also been more sharply defined to meet specific federal policy objectives. Its legislation was amended then, so that its programme objectives became more clearly integrated with those government policies, and also in terms of organisational accountabilities.

But, at the time of writing (2003), federal government policy towards the original public service broadcaster, the ABC, was still ambiguous, perhaps deliberately so. A 1981 report had made a major contribution to long-overdue policy development, and its implementing legislation of 1983 had provided the ABC with a statutory charter and other statutory guidelines, which went a long way to help the organisation become more efficient and more relevant to the needs of the last quarter of the 20th century.

But all of this predated the information communications technology (ICT) era of the late 1980s, and so a reappraisal of those statutory objectives to bring them more in line with the new needs of the 21st century is overdue. The Mansfield inquiry, set up by the conservative John Howard government, issued a report in 1997 (*The challenge of a better ABC*) which went a long way towards pushing those policy choices forward, still within the "values" ethic. Currently, it seems, they have been quietly shelved (Appendix 3 (d) (iii)).

Meanwhile a series of ad-hoc, tactical, budget-driven decisions by successive governments of both the political left and right during the last decade of the 20th century were seen by some to have eroded the corporation's ability to deliver pro-grammes successfully fulfilling core values objectives. Since these decisions included major cuts to the ABC's external broadcasting services, they seemed to demonstrate a lack of understanding by Australia's decision-makers about the inter-play between key domestic and external policies. They also sidestepped the need for an update of the ABC's Act, including its charter provisions, to match the more integrated policy approach already provided to the SBS.

A reluctance to pay the price of a democratic institution, which should per-haps be seen as a percentage of Gross Domestic Product (GDP), led inevitably to the overt semi-commercialisation of the SBS and covert moves to commercialise the ABC, which seemed to be gathering strength at the turn of the century.

So Australian political leaders, as well as those in other Western democracies, could well re-visit global and regional policy frameworks already provided by bodies such as the United Nations and the EU (see: Appendixes). In terms of state-level policy and implementation responses to globalisation, they could well look at the Canadian model, too.

There are always plenty of internal critics of existing policies and structures, and I share the concerns of those who see continuing "unresolved contradictions" about the role of public broadcasting in a globalised world. But Australian gov-ernments, I think, can meet their citizenship obligations through a relative fine-tuning of existing policies, rather than by needing to undertake major reforms.

Programme importers: Ireland and New Zealand: the need for reform

That isn't the case, however, with the smaller and more vulnerable Western democracies of Ireland and New Zealand. As with Canada and Australia, there are some parallels between them. Each has espoused the free market ideology in varying degrees; each has decades of history serving as producers of primary agri-cultural products for the British market. They both have small popula-tions—New Zealand, four million, Ireland, now close to that—and they've been facing similar problems stemming from rapid economic and social change in the last quarter of the 20th century.

But partly because of differing historical and cultural traditions and partly because their governments have made different strategic, political and economic choices, their communications policy responses differed significantly. These have been of sufficient scale to make the different status of the democratic role of their public broadcasters noticeable too. But as the twin pressures of globalisation and the market intensify, the gap between future policy options for both these small Western democracies is narrowing. In each case, a political recognition of the need for a new definition of public service broadcasting to help re-vitalise their own forms of democracy will be of critical importance.

Ireland: a constitutional link

Ireland, a small state on the periphery of Western Europe, has, I think, been able to cope relatively well so far in meeting the citizenship needs of its people through its communications policies though, at the end of 2003, it seemed to be on the brink of watershed policy decisions.

As I see it, Ireland's current strengths to date stem from three historical factors.

First, Ireland's population was until very recently homogenous to an unusual degree on a world scale, and so its people have a high level of shared values. While it took a long political struggle for Ireland to regain the independence it had lost through its integration into the United Kingdom in 1801, it did finally succeed. The Irish Free State was established in 1922, and its sovereign status was taken a step further when it became the Republic of Ireland in 1949, severing all remaining formal ties with Britain.

Second, this time frame meant that the coincidental arrival of radio in the 1920s was inevitably bound up with the early constitutional and legislative efforts to re-build the state on the cultural foundations of an ancient Celtic nation. In turn, the introduction of television in the 1960s was closely linked to political and economic decisions building the foundations of the current, modern Ireland, which began when Sean Lemass succeeded the veteran Eamon de Valera as taoiseach (prime minister) from 1959–66 (Appendix 3 (e) (ii)).

Third, Irish membership in the European Economic Community (now, the European Union) in 1973 placed it under the umbrella of a supra-national body, which gave successive Irish governments easy access to evolving EU-wide communications policies reflecting the values of Western liberal democracy.

◆   ◆   ◆

A major step in the rebuilding of the Irish state was the adoption of a new constitution in 1937, one seen largely as the work of de Valera, leader of the Fianna Fail ("Warriors of Ireland") party he had founded in 1926. The constitution was aimed primarily at redefining Ireland's relationship with Britain, but it also set the framework for internal state-building in the increasingly turbulent decade of 1930s Europe, and for the national public service broadcaster Radio Éireann. While article 8.1 enshrined the Irish language as "the national language and the national first language of the state," article 40 guaranteed the right of citizens "to express freely their convictions and opinions…subject to public order and morality (Appendix 3 (e) (i)).

The introduction of television into Ireland soon after Sean Lemass came to power in 1959 can be more clearly seen in retrospect for having been, as one analyst puts it, "…a major instrument in the conversion to consumerism." Lemass's decision, though, ended a decade of doubts about the various policy options. An inevitable split had developed between advocates of the U.S.-style "business" model and the West European-style "values" model. This was a reflection of the eternal conflict between private rights and the public good, with the department of finance, probably like finance departments and treasuries of all times and in all countries, favouring the business model as the one least likely to lead to an ongoing exposure to financial risk for Irish governments.

But, in the end, and importantly, ownership of the first television service was denied to overseas commercial interests, and so a strong element of political control over policy choices was preserved for the future. The outcome, a hybrid system financed partly by a licence fee set by the government, and partly by advertising revenues, was hailed as "an Irish solution to an Irish problem," and it's continued that way ever since. Eventually, Radio Éireann was renamed Radio Telefís Éireann, the present-day RTÉ, seen by Lemass and his successors as "an instrument of public policy and as such responsible to the government."

A significant development came in the *Broadcasting Authority (Amendment) Act 1976*. Its section 13 is the nearest there is to a statutory charter for RTÉ. It specifically introduced a cross-reference to the democratic values set out in the Irish constitution and obliged RTÉ to help form public awareness of the values and traditions of other countries, especially those in the EEC/EU (Appendix 3 (e) (iii)).

This last reference, coming only three years after Ireland achieved EEC/EU membership, foreshadowed a later pattern of deliberate political decisions to apply many EU policies, even though some of them aren't mandatory on state governments. The Irish government, for example, chose to give the EU's *Television without frontiers* directive (Appendix 2 (b)) legal status by passing a statutory instrument two years later, giving it force within Ireland.

Ireland's constitutional, political and successful economic background has enabled RTÉ to retain an influential role in a challenging era. Like other public service broadcasters in Western democracies, though, it's had its "thrills and chills" as an interface between the politicians and the public, especially in the first four decades of its television service. That's why I favour the further protection of a charter provision in legislation, both setting out for the politicians, the public and broadcasters alike, a range of broad programming objectives, and at the same time usefully consolidating a string of previous enactments. Some examples are given in the Appendixes.

Charter provisions like these, I think, go a step further than the foundations already in RTÉ's current governing legislation because they can acknowledge public service broadcasting's overarching role as part of the democratic process, including what's widely labelled as "education for citizenship." They usually also identify the public need for local programme content to balance the U.S.-dominated mass-appeal entertainment provided by an increasing number of private sector satellite and cable distribution services.

A highly relevant rationale for such a move was set out in an Irish government Green (discussion) Paper in 1995 (*Active or passive? Broadcasting in the future tense*). This recognised that faster rates of change stemming from the impetus of globalisation had caused "a profound rupture between present and past." In this new context it saw broadcasting as "strongly charged with opposite meanings of promise and threat." The promise included "becoming the motor of modernisation, cultural innovation, social transformation, even democratisation." The threat, it said bluntly, included "pitting profit motive against collective rights, deterritorialised imperialism against minority cultural needs."

But, after a change of government, it came as no surprise when this discussion paper, which I think raised important issues relevant to Ireland's 21st century future, was dropped. The political merry-go-round started again with a new government and a new inquiry called *The Forum on Broadcasting*, set up partly because RTÉs revenues were inevitably falling as the small Irish communications market became more fragmented and more competitive.

By the end of 2003 there were ominous signs that the government was moving against the public interest. Its *Broadcasting (Funding) Bill 2003* proposed diverting licence fee finance away from RTÉ and instead routing it through a distributive body. This is like the flawed New Zealand system where, for nearly two decades, a government organisation branding itself as *New Zealand On Air* has been using public finance to commission some local programming for CanWest, a private sector television company which also operates in Ireland. The result, of course, has been to diminish the amount of finance available to enable public sector broadcasters to fulfil their role. It has also added further confusion to the mixture of public and private sector objectives already existing in a hybrid system.

So I think that the urgent threshold issue for Irish governments now and in the immediate future is to ensure a better balance, a better range of genuine choice, for the Irish people. This can be achieved if they redefine the purpose of RTÉ in charter legislation; then decide that the country can afford a more clearly complementary, rather than a partly competitive (because part commercially financed) public service television channel to help make it all happen. Since Ireland has earned the title of "the Celtic tiger" for its economic performance in recent decades, I think it could, and should, be afforded.

But if the balance tips the other way Ireland, like New Zealand, will end up at the bottom of the slippery slope of business values. Instead of being a model for other small countries, the Irish system will become another warning.

New Zealand: How far can market failure be modified?

New Zealand, a Western state on the southern rim of the Pacific Ocean, is a small state that is truly peripheral in a global geographic sense, having some of the longest trade routes in the world. It also has a strong Polynesian foundation, with its Maori people making up some fifteen percent of its population. From its establishment as a British colony following the *Treaty of Waitangi* with Maori in 1840, it became highly dependant on agricultural trade with Britain, especially after the introduction of refrigerated cargo ships in 1882. Those economic and cultural ties were inevitably weakened when Britain eventually achieved membership of the EEC/EU in 1973, the same year as Ireland, after a decade of trying.

Because of their relatively small populations, New Zealand's often compared with Ireland by economic analysts, although other small countries, like Denmark, could also be used for purposes of comparison. In my context, I think that the differences between New Zealand and Ireland are more important than the perceived similarities.

One difference, not often identified or debated but, I think a relevant historical factor, is that unlike Ireland, New Zealand didn't have to fight for its independence. In fact, almost the reverse happened: when this status was offered under Britain's *Statute of Westminster 1931* New Zealand took its time, delaying ratification until 1947. It can be argued that legally this is its year of independent statehood, although, in practise, this had been tacitly assumed throughout the first half of the 20th century.

Nor does New Zealand have a written constitution, though this might well come about if future governments decide that the country should break its remaining ties with the British monarchy and become a democratic republic within the British Commonwealth, like India. In the closing years of the 20th century, though, even a suggestion by a former prime minister that a process be agreed for looking at the concept of a written constitution had been brushed aside.

Of course, another major difference is that, again unlike Ireland, New Zealand didn't have the option of EU membership in 1973. New Zealand's response to its economic challenges in the 1980s and 1990s was to adopt the free market ideology more vigorously than other players. By 1998 it was ranked on top of a world chart calculating the rate of change towards economic liberalism since 1985, while Ireland was ranked only seventeenth. But on a global ranking of wealth on a gross domestic product (GDP) per capita basis, New Zealand had been overtaken by Denmark as long ago as 1965, despite the costs of Denmark's strong commitment to a welfare state, and by Ireland in 1990, despite, at that stage, six years of New Zealand's economic experiment.

By the 1980s and the 1990s the switch away from a primary strategic and economic linkage with Britain had been echoed by a weakening of cultural affiliations with Britain. By the start of the 21st century for many New Zealanders, and for most of the under-forties, the "children of the free market," the culture they most admired and sought to emulate was American. This trend was reinforced by political decisions to adopt the U.S. business model for a communications industry that was virtually un-regulated from the late 1980s onwards. However, unlike the U.S., all restrictions on foreign ownership were removed. As a consequence, these cultural shifts were reinforced by the market-driven programme strategies of new channels, owned or controlled by transnationals like Rupert Murdoch's NewsCorp or Canada's CanWest.

◆   ◆   ◆

Like Ireland, though, New Zealand's historical approach to communications policies has led to dual commercial and social objectives: through separate organisations in the radio-only days of the 1920s, then through a variety of hybrid state-run organisational structures following the arrival of television in 1960. These, as in Ireland, offered a reasonable enough service for a while, though real choices deteriorated sharply as successive governments made the television service increasingly commercialised.

A fundamental flaw in all of this, I think, is that the many structural changes to its public broadcasting bodies took place in a constitutional and strategic political vacuum. The story of New Zealand public service broadcasting is a story of mixed objectives and of missed opportunities to separate out commercial and public service functions, despite policy advice from myself and, no doubt, others. As one communications analyst put it, the interplay between politics and broadcasting has been shaped "far more by political circumstances and opportunism than by principled beliefs and commitment."

The state's role in the provision of television services hit rock bottom in 1988, when Television New Zealand (TVNZ) was redefined as a state-owned enterprise (SOE) under free market legislation having only financial performance objectives and no programming objectives at all. Unfortunately, though, the politicians forgot to tell the public explicitly that this is what was intended. The public certainly hadn't been asked for its views about any such change, through a widely-advertised or extensive public consultation process. Nor had it been asked what its needs were, either as consumers or as citizens.

It was no surprise, then, that a decade later TVNZ was being described by government-appointed business analysts as having no non-commercial components whatsoever, but "a purely commercial programme strategy." And so, after opting out of public service television as it is generally understood for the better part of a generation, by the turn of the century a centre-right government was on the brink of putting it up for sale to the private sector. It was saved for the public only by a change back to a centre-left Labour government. So, in New Zealand, at the start of the new century, the market still rules, in broadcasting as in everything else, although attempts were being made, somewhat late in the day, to mitigate some of the worst consequences of market failure.

For public service broadcasters, this meant a charter for the wholly non-commercial Radio New Zealand in 1995, followed eight years later by one for the highly-commercial TVNZ in 2003 (Appendixes 3 (f) (iv) and (v)). TVNZ, however, is still burdened with a built-in conflict between commercial and social objectives. The 2003 legislation retains a dual obligation for TVNZ to maintain its commercial performance, which incredibly includes returning a dividend to the government of the day, while, at the same time, seeking to give effect to its charter.

Whether this will prove to be enough has yet to be tested. I think the commercial culture is now so embedded that one more structural change is still needed: to amalgamate TVNZ, RNZ and a long-promised Maori television service into a single, non-commercial body financed entirely by government grants. Things have gone so far that a statutory charter by itself might not be enough.

However, how the mitigating steps taken in 2003 will work out in practice, or how future governments deal with the public role in evolving communications policies, will help determine the future quality of democracy in a small state in the Pacific hemisphere where major power shifts are likely to develop in the first quarter of the 21st century.

By 2025, New Zealand's extensive maritime Exclusive Economic Zone and its geographic position as one of only a handful of "gateway" states with claims in Antarctica might well have greater strategic significance than it does today. Its ability to influence its Pacific neighbours through advocacy of democratic values could also turn on external perceptions of how New Zealand handles its own democratic institutions at home.

◆   ◆   ◆

By the start of the 21st century, both Ireland and New Zealand were importing more television programmes than a decade earlier.

3

World and regional policy frameworks

World responses: UNESCO: a Cold War "battered baby"

Today's global and regional public policies on communications can be tracked back in a continuous thread to the outcomes of the French and American revolutions of the 18th century.

The first formal affirmation of the principle of freedom of information is in the French *Declaration of the Rights of Man and of the Citizen* of 1789. Its Article XI describes 'the free communication of ideas and opinions' as "one of the most precious rights of man (sic)," and says that, in consequence, every citizen "can freely speak, write and print subject to responsibility for the abuse of this freedom in the cases determined by law."

The First Amendment to the US constitution, quoted so often, came a couple of years later in 1791 (Appendix 3 (a) (i)). During the Second World War, 150 years later, U.S. President Roosevelt placed "freedom of speech and expression everywhere in the world" in a 1941 declaration of war aims.

The main post-war forum for communications policy debate, apart from the UN General Assembly, has been the UN Educational, Scientific and Cultural Organisation (UNESCO). Its 1945 constitution reflects the Western commitment to "advancing the mutual knowledge and understanding of peoples" through international agreements designed to promote the "free flow of ideas by word and image" (Article II 2 (a)). These principles were strengthened by Article 19 of the *UN Declaration of Human Rights 1948*: "Everyone has the right to freedom of opinion and expression; this right includes freedom to hold opinions without interference and to seek, receive and impart information and ideas through any media and regardless of frontiers" (Appendix 1 (a)).

The same principles, in turn, were reinforced by the *UN International Covenant on Civil and Political Rights 1966*. Its Article 19 echoes that of the Human Rights Declaration, but then extends it by specifying that the right to "seek, receive and impart information and ideas" refers not just to "any media," (as in the Human Rights Declaration) but "either orally, in writing or in print, in the form of art, or through any media of his (sic) choice" (Appendix 1 (b)).

The covenant has so far been ratified by some ninety states which have, therefore, had a ready-made opportunity to co-ordinate and promote a vertically integrated set of global "rights" policies within their domestic legislation if they wanted to.

The U.S.: out and back

On the global scale it was inevitable, I suppose, that the issue of information flows became one of the arenas for ideological confrontation during the Cold War years. The expression "free flow of information" synthesised the policy position of the West, led by the U.S. Against this the Eastern bloc states, led by the former Soviet Union, argued for a controlled flow of information, based on international agreements and respecting the principle of non-interference in the domestic affairs of states. And the non-aligned developing countries identified a third issue: the imbalance of information between the developed North and the developing South. The Soviet bloc and non-aligned nations saw their positions as being complementary and so they joined forces both in the U.N. itself and within UNESCO, calling at the end of the 1970s for a *New World Information and Communication Order (NWICO)*.

As UNESCO itself records, discussions on the three differing approaches to a global communications policy became "extremely stormy," leading first the U.S. (1984) and then Britain (1985) to pull out from UNESCO. Britain rejoined in 1997, but the U.S. didn't do so until 1 October, 2003.

I think even this belated return of the U.S. is potentially good news for all of us. This is because the emergence of even a tentative form of democracy within the transitional states of both the former Soviet Union and the Third World means that these states are also moving, however slowly and erratically, towards the Western concepts of freedom of expression and media independence. So Western countries surely need to be active members of a global forum, set up in part to promote the free flow of ideas, and engage themselves fully in future debates.

The idealist in me hopes that this could result in all member-states looking at their societies from a more plural perspective, and then providing more balanced communications policies and systems to help achieve this goal. The realist in me, however, acknowledges that the new major private sector world companies have already gained an edge by having world communications politics placed in their preferred forum of the World Trade Organisation (WTO), a body committed to maximising the freedom of market forces. For them, this was something of a coup.

But if the West wants to continue to advocate human rights and the democratic form of government worldwide, (although Huntington and others believe that democracy is probably not a universal system of government), then it's surely in its interests to engage in the debate within global institutions like UNESCO. It should also contribute expertise to give the more open communications systems in the transitional democracies a better chance of survival and development.

In tandem with this, the West should put its own domestic communications systems into better order, within the context of global policy frameworks, to help counter apathy at home and perhaps to re-invigorate their own forms of democracy. Its advocacy to others would then also become more credible.

The new agenda

Many of the communications imbalances identified by UNESCO during the Cold War years are still there and still need to be addressed, but with a fresh pair of eyes, looking from the perspective of current and future possibilities. The "private v public sector" debate is now the old agenda: the new agenda is not so much "globalisation v the state," but finding a redefined role for the state in an increasingly globalised world.

The historical imbalances had already been the focus of a *UNESCO Mass Media Declaration 1978,* passed unanimously, including support from the U.S., then still a member (Appendix 1 (c)). It was followed by an international commission on communications problems chaired by Sean MacBride. Its report, *Many voices, one world* was tabled at UNESCO's 1980 conference. By then, though, the fragile consensus within UNESCO was wearing thin and these two events contributed to the eventual U.S. and British withdrawals from the organisation.

But the report did broaden the Human Rights Declaration's "right to information" by an extension of these specific rights into a new concept: the more interactive "right to communicate." This broader definition began to be seen during the 1990s as central to the human rights debate, and so a valid subject for discussion about ways to achieve a more balanced and democratic dialogue between states. And I would add it was also a valid subject for discussion about ways to achieve a more democratic dialogue *within* states, including the existing democracies and especially their smaller members.

UNESCO took advantage of the "beginning of the end" of the Cold War to adopt an amended communications strategy in 1989, the year the Berlin wall fell. This strategy has three prongs: a reaffirmation of UNESCO's constitutional obligation to promote the free flow of information; marrying this with the NWICO goal of seeking a "wider and better balanced flow," but this time with the significant difference that this should be compatible with the "free flow" principle; and finally, seeking to improve the capacity of developing countries to take part in the communications revolution.

But policy, even global policy; and perhaps *especially* global policy, is one thing; sustained and equal implementation of global policy is another.

By the time of its 1997 report UNESCO had to record that international aid for communications had lagged well behind other forms of aid to the transitional democracies, noting: "It is difficult to imagine that only a few crumbs remain to consolidate the achievements of democracy in the communications field, since it is well known that the media were and are still in Europe, as in other regions of the world, the driving force behind the transition to democracy."

But at a regional level, only some groupings of states have explicit communications policies, and some of those that do exist are showing patchy results, even within the older democracies of Western Europe.

Regional responses: Europe v. "the giants"

The most comprehensive attempt to date to coordinate policy responses at a regional inter-government level to the globalisation/Americanisation of the electronic media market has been made by the European Union, which over the years has addressed different aspects of the issue from a variety of perspectives. In many ways these EU initiatives had their historical genesis in a long-standing battle led by the France of President de Gaulle against what he saw in the 1960s as an increasing threat to France's, and ultimately Europe's, cultural identity from strong Anglo-Saxon (primarily US/UK) cultural, including television programme, sources.

Although there are other charters and declarations—for example, in the Americas (1969) and in Africa (1981)—the EU model is certainly the best known and cumulatively the most comprehensive. Of the other major trading blocs, the North American Free Trade Area (NAFTA) rules don't apply to cultural industries, while the Asia Pacific Economic Cooperation (APEC) group was beginning to consider the impacts of global communications only in late 1999.

But in the EU the central importance of their historical values-driven public service model was recognised in a protocol annexed to the original *Treaty of Amsterdam* instituting the Community, while the role of such broadcasters has been linked to human rights obligations through article 10 of the *European Convention on Human Rights* passed as far back as 1950.

The outcomes of a more recent European ministerial conference on mass media policy in 1994 are important on three principal grounds. First, they formally moved the rationale for public service broadcasting on from the 1920s, paternalistic, "It's a good idea and good for you" approach to an explicit linkage with the values of democratic societies, and especially human rights. Second, because they set out what is in effect a mission statement for public service broadcasters. Third, because they recommend that all EU member-states guarantee "at least one comprehensive wide-range programme service comprising information, education, culture and entertainment *(note the order)* which is accessible to all members of the public." (See Appendix 2a).

And, of course, its principles are readily portable to other countries as the basis for policy development, whether members of the EU or not.

The new "planetary war"

More recently still, a high-level group providing the first outline of a European audiovisual policy for the 21st century began by stating that its 1998 report was based on the "incontestable premise" that a modern democratic society can't exist without communications media, which among other objectives, "provide the means whereby the public debate which underpins free and democratic societies can take place, means that the market will not necessarily deliver on its own."

It contrasts the West European preference for a balance between the market and the role of the state with the competitive approach taken by the U.S. like this: "It has never been assumed in Europe that the broadcasting and audiovisual sector should be treated as an economic subject only, or that the market would, per se, guarantee a pluralistic service...a core element of European broadcasting policies has always been to educate and inform the viewer, over and above purely commercial considerations." And education and training for the digital age, it says, must mean that individual governments should give greater importance to teaching media literacy in schools, so that individuals will be able to overcome the information overload.

Meanwhile, EU television-specific policy has been developed, and will almost certainly develop further, from a 1989 Directive, the *Television without frontiers* policy, which was modified in 1997 chiefly to guarantee public access to major national or international events such as the Olympic Games, part of the EU's ongoing efforts to balance the public interest with the development of the market.

The directives are part of an ongoing EU strategy to create a common cultural market, able to guarantee both the survival of European cultural identity and its industry competitiveness.

And in 1999 a Council of Europe recommendation tackled ways in which member-states could promote a variety of media choices, especially for information. It suggested a range of policy options, including legislation to define thresholds to limit the influence that a single commercial company or group might have in the overall marketplace; the introduction of rules to minimise the negative impact of networking; and subsidies for media bodies printing or broadcasting in a minority language (for extracts from key documents, see: Appendixes 2 (a), (b) and (c)).

Even so, a joint UNESCO/EC assessment of the effectiveness of the 1989 television directives, some ten years after their introduction, recorded that all the major established channels within the EU, whether public or private, had been distracted from their primary policy objectives. This was because of the need to fight a different "war," a battle for audience share of the increasingly fragmenting market caused by the combination of free market deregulation and new technologies, a "planetary war," with the trans-national multi-media programme supply corporations seeking a significant market share to maximise advertising and subscription revenues.

The inevitable outcome was a widespread adoption by all programme providers, public as well as private, of competitive programming strategies, rather than the broadly complementary scheduling strategies of even the 1980s. The equally inevitable result was that cultural and other more-demanding programmes, where they remained at all, were being progressively pushed into low-viewing slots, like the mornings and late evenings. Not surprisingly, if somewhat hopefully, the study urged the public channels to try to ensure that the future television landscape "is not completely given over to the law of the market."

The market, of course, was not expected to meet these wider viewer needs at all. Nor does it.

Wanted: a "political architecture" for communications

One of the tests of a democracy is whether governments put in place, as a deliberate piece of political architecture, a system of human communications structured so that their citizens can be well-informed, develop their own opinions and express them without fear of losing their jobs, let alone a fear of being arrested or shot, and so participate more fully in the core democratic right of political choice.

This doesn't apply only to the emerging democracies of the former Soviet Union and of the Third World. There has to be evidence of a similar deliberate structure within Western states, too, if they want to meet their human rights obligations to their own citizens and so be taken seriously as models by others.

This is the key matrix against which the effectiveness of democratic government in Western states should be re-assessed and then judged.

For democratic choice to be achievable there must be an overall policy framework enabling the operation of traditional, mainstream media—print, radio and television—independently of governments and political parties. Where relevant and cost-effective, new technologies also should be used as a form of distribution.

"Teledemocracy"—or real involvement?

Historically, the wish to demonstrate democratic choice has embraced the concept of a publicly-owned broadcasting system. But the public service has to be delivered in such a way as to provide both for shared experiences and for a real involvement in democratic process, not just the illusion offered by the current vogue for the instant phone-in polls of "teledemocracy."

Public service broadcasting has existed both as a concept and as a fact for more than seventy years and has a well-recorded history. While there may well be a number of opinions about the year-by-year interpretation of the concept in a rapidly-changing world, there is a remarkable degree of consistency about the goals of public service broadcasting, based on the BBC's original trilogy of "to inform, educate and entertain."

One of the better-known definitions of public service broadcasting comes from the Broadcasting Research Unit (BRU), a now-defunct independent body originally jointly sponsored by the BBC, the British film industry, the former Independent Broadcasting Authority (IBA) of Britain, and the Markle Foundation of New York. It identified eight main principles:

- Geographic universality—programmes should be made available to the whole population.

- Universal appeal—programmes should cater for all interests and tastes.

- Minorities, especially disadvantaged minorities, should receive particular provision.

- Broadcasters should recognise their special relationship to the sense of national identity and community.

- Broadcasting should be distanced from all special interests, and in particular those of the government of the day.

- Universality of payment—one main instrument of broadcasting should be financed by all users.

- Broadcasting should be structured to encourage competition in good programming, rather than competition for numbers.

- The public guidelines for broadcasting should be designed to liberate, rather than restrict, the programme makers.

A more explicit values-driven approach has been set out by another group, the thirty-member Public Broadcasters International (PBI), which is sponsored by Canada's TVOntario and Japan's NHK. They described public service broadcasting as "marked by the highest values—not the values of the market place alone nor the values of any particular government—but those values which give highest priority to the needs of citizens to be informed, educated and entertained." More specifically they saw such broadcasting as "enriching the human experience;" as "an indispensable instrument for the strengthening of democracy;" as a vehicle to promote "cultural richness and diversity;" and as having a "moral responsibility" to provide children as well as adults with "reliable and trustworthy programs of integrity." All of this was further defined in an agreed nine-point mission statement (Appendix 1 (d)).

Taken together, the BRU principles, set out in 1986, and the PBI values provide a strong rationale for redefining in policy terms the role expected from existing or new public service broadcasters.

"Tyranny of the market"

Yet the keen appreciation by the media and the public of the potential for political pressure on public service broadcasters in the days of monopoly, or more controlled competition, hasn't been matched by an equally keen concern to identify, monitor and debate the pressures of the market on those same bodies. As the joint editors of a UN study, *The changing nature of democracy,* put it: "In many respects, the tyranny of the market seems much stronger than the tyranny of the state these days."

An important step towards the regeneration of democracy within the West, therefore, is not only the provision of a range of information as a public service, but a redefinition of what that range should encompass day-by-day.

I think that a 1997 report on Australia's ABC, the Mansfield Report, *The challenges of a better ABC,* came close to the mark when recommending that the ABC's statutory requirement to maintain a news and information service to cover current events should now be broadened. The information needs of a democratic and pluralist society, it said, extend beyond the need to be informed about current events: "It is also important that citizens have access to information, commentary and debate on issues of public importance in the broadest sense. These include scientific and technological developments, issues of public policy, health, education, religious and legal matters."

A widespread acceptance by Western governments of this contemporary definition of information, or something similar, together with a redefinition of how best to meet society's changing needs for education, would help restore the original programming balance between public service broadcasters and the consumer-driven market.

Until that happens, the overall market will remain asymmetrical.

A revised contract between governments and public service broadcasters, settling for the provision of these traditional services, but in new, multi-media ways and using a parcel of performance measures not driven by the purely commercial measurement of audience ratings, would help both to mitigate the impact of the transnational consumer-driven communications market on the democratic process and perhaps encourage stronger citizen participation in democracy as well.

◆   ◆   ◆

I recognise that UN and EU communications policies and the ways in which they are implemented in some countries at some times are not without their critics, whether from academics, state-level policy-makers or individual practitioners. But good broadcasting, like good health, is often taken for granted and valued properly only once it's lost. The range and quality of these global and regional media policies, taken together, do offer an existing policy framework for governments willing to reinvigorate their domestic institutions.

One of the important debates facing the next generation, a debate *within* states as well as *between* states, is going to be about human rights. But there's no need for policy-makers to reinvent the wheel if they decide to act more convincingly in this area. There's a wide range of existing global and regional policy frameworks for individual states to draw from. There just has to be the political will to do so.

4

Making it happen: Britain's Channel Four, Canada's TVOntario, Australia's SBS

Small is beautiful

I've never understood why policy advisers to governments seem obsessed with Britain's BBC, Canada's CBC and Australia's ABC as potential models of public service broadcasting in their home territories, unless it's a deliberate ploy by officials to demonstrate to politicians and the public what *isn't* affordable at home, especially in the fifty or so UN-member states having populations of five million or less.

The key to successful policy development and planning, as in much else, is surely relevance. Smaller countries might be about the same size as the state of Arizona, not the whole of the U.S.; their population somewhere between that of Wales or Scotland, not that of Britain as a whole; and their per capita income closer to that of other smaller states, like Ireland. So approaches that work as a cost-effective alternative public service broadcaster, like Britain's Channel Four; or work in a single Canadian province, like Ontario, or that meet the needs of specific policy objectives within a middle-ranking country like Australia, will have more relevance than models appropriate for bigger or richer states. That's why this chapter will look at the work of Britain's Channel Four, Canada's TVOntario, and Australia's Special Broadcasting Service (SBS).

From a zero-based, clean sheet of paper approach, elements of these working models, each proven over twenty to thirty years, could be adapted also as part of the policy options for bigger states.

Channel Four—no longer "a bore"

Britain's Channel Four has long been a model for the commissioning approach to innovative programme-making, so keeping its own overheads relatively low while at the same time stimulating private sector employment and providing a prime time showcase for local emerging entertainment talent, including film makers. It also shows how public sector television can be one hundred percent commercially-financed and yet deliver complementary programming.

◆   ◆   ◆

When Margaret (later Lady) Thatcher's Conservative government set up Channel Four in Britain in 1982, it gave it a remarkably wide statutory mandate: "to encourage innovation and experiment in the form and content of programmes;" to cater for interests not already provided by the other, bigger channels making up the private sector Independent Television (ITV) service, the other half of what was then widely referred to as the "cosy duopoly" with the BBC at that time, and above all to provide "a distinctive service"—in other words, to be different. Just how different was left in the first instance to the broadcasters themselves.

Its founding chief executive, Jeremy (now, Sir Jeremy) Isaacs, has recalled that the early schedules annoyed politicians on both the left and the right; some of the latter, he says, had been expecting programmes of minority interest to be just for golfers and yachties, rather than also about homosexuals or immigrant communities. Newspaper critics of the time had a field day. Murdoch's *The Sun* trumpeted, "Channel Bore, Channel Snore, Channel Four-letter word." During a lunch meeting in those early days with the British Home Secretary and chief architect of the Channel Four legislation, Willie (later Lord) Whitelaw, Isaacs says he put the case that people needed to get things off their chest, and that freedom to speak out could pre-empt violent demonstration for change. He records: "Willie took another sip of Chablis, rolled his eyes and agreed there was something to be said for it."

So a channel brought into being in the early days of a government headed by a hard-line economic neo-liberal prime minister saw life and survived its first stormy months partly because of the tolerance of a politically-liberal Conservative Party minister.

Commercial—but complementary—competition

However it turned out in its early days, the idea behind Channel Four was that it should break the mould within the existing private sector and offer not only more competition but also more genuine, complementary choice. Central to the achievement of this objective was the requirement that an already-established and respected commercial television news service, ITN, should be carried by the new channel but complemented by programmes made as far as possible by independent producers rather than produced in-house.

This it has done so successfully that this aspect of its work has since been taken as a model for Ireland's Telefis na Gaeilge (T na G) Gaelic channel. In its report on its own activities in the closing years of the 20th century, Channel Four was able to record that fifty-six percent of programming was commissioned from as many as 465 independent producers, balanced by forty-four percent of programmes acquired, chiefly from ITV channels and international markets. All of this, plus a new subscription film channel and Internet services, delivered by some 700 staff and regularly achieving a ratings share in an increasingly competitive market of about ten percent, reaching (being sampled by) about eighty-five percent of the total British population each week; and returning financial profits.

The channel had been launched in 1982 with funds coming substantially from government levies charged against the ITV companies, and from commercial income sold by them on the fledgling channel's behalf. However, Channel Four took responsibility for its own advertising sales in 1993 and has since performed well in three target markets sought by advertisers: not just the sixteen-to-twenty-four-year-olds, but also the more elusive ABC1 socio-demographic group and the even more elusive group of light commercial viewers.

If a public service television channel has to be financed from advertising, either wholly or partially, then the Channel Four experience confirms that viability can be achieved from a wider range of programming targeted at older viewers and advertising drawn from their discretionary spending patterns, classically including travel, cars, household white goods and insurance, all typically spent after mortgages have been paid off and children have left home.

So one aspect of the Channel Four story that has special significance for other states is that its different programming and sales strategies have worked. In fact, it has given the British government such proof of its long-term financial viability that a scheme originally devised to withhold a percentage of its annual revenue as a sort of insurance policy against company failure, could be phased out in 1998 and ended completely in 1999. Savings from the first phase helped in the launch of a new film channel, called Film Four, and distributed by digital transmission.

A new century, a new deal

And, of even more significance for this study, the liberation of funds was part of a package that included a more specific programme brief as part of a revised licence issued by Britain's relatively light touch regulator, the Independent Television Commission (ITC). In effect, when combined with its legislative framework, this amounted to a new contract with the state. Releasing its decision, the ITC described Channel Four as a "highly valued public service broadcaster with a difference. Accentuating that difference has been at the core of revising its licence" (Appendix 3 (b) (iii).

A statement of programme policy, drawn up by Channel Four to show how it aimed to implement the new conditions, said it had already been providing public service and 'creative competition' for the BBC as well as for the mainstream commercial channels, its original terms of reference. And it said the new licence would meet its aspirations to broaden its role further still in the 21st century by defining its role in a multi-channel environment in relation to all channels serving the British viewer, including the relatively new satellite channels like Murdoch's BSkyB. Setting the framework for realistic political and public expectations of its future performance in ratings terms, projected to hover around eight to ten percent even as the market fragments further in the first years of the new century, the paper recalled that while some of its programmes would aim to attract large numbers, it had never been expected to be a mass audience channel.

Its 21st century role, in effect an amplification of its originally legislation, would be to "encourage pluralism, provide a favoured place for the untried, and encourage innovation in style, content, perspective and talent"—especially new talent.

Key to its ability to provide genuine choice from other channels, it said, was the provision of programmes not available on those channels, so offering viewers greater variety in subject matter "in the pursuit of serious themes and in the treatment and length of programmes." It would also offer them at "accessible times in the schedules."

Exactly. These questions of overall tone, style of presentation and length, not only of the programmes themselves, but also of interview segments within them that allow complete thoughts to be conveyed and digested rather than edited down to microscopic sound bites—these are some of the intangible ways in which even a commercially-financed public service channel can be readily distinguished by viewers from a commercially-financed business operation. Another is the commitment to offer genuine choice at accessible times in the schedules.

Neither of these important elements can work in a fully, or largely, deregulated market environment, especially for channels wholly or partly financed from commercial sources. Programmes will then increasingly be broadcast in prime time *only* if they fit within the straitjacket of advertiser-driven presentational and content criteria. In the scramble for ratings, anything else is driven to the viewing wastelands of daytime or late night, often post-midnight, television.

Monitoring a democratic institution

For its part Channel Four sees itself as meeting the newly agreed goals by careful scheduling and presentation as much as by programme selection and content. In these ways, it says, it "can and should make a contribution to a plural and democratic society."

And, of course, in the overall British communications industry context, the ITC has been there to monitor actual performance and to make sure that the commercial channels live up to their combined statutory and licence remits (in 2003, though, it was in process of being merged with four other regulatory bodies).

This level of light regulation is a pivotal element of a communications industry policy package. It reassures the government that it's receiving the services it either pays for (the non-commercial model), or allows into the market place on specific terms (like Channel Four, or Ireland's RTÉ). It reassures the public that a body with more time and expertise than any individual or community group can possibly have, is looking after the public interest. And it means that the broadcasters and their governing bodies know exactly where they stand.

People can, and will, make use of complaints procedures, but that's not the same thing. The ITC's monitoring system, for example, is both inclusive and open: inclusive in that it takes account of comments from its own Viewer Consultative Councils; open in that its sometimes fairly blunt findings are published annually.

Of course there's a cost to the state in setting up and maintaining even a broad-brush monitoring system of industry programme output. But again, from a governmental perspective, isn't transparency of accounting against agreed performance measures what it's all about? And from the public's perspective, isn't this an acceptable price to pay for an open system of auditing the programme output of an important democratic and national cultural identity institution?

TVOntario: anticipating the "knowledge economy"

TVOntario's experiences as a multi-media learning resource, broadcasting sixty percent of local content, and with seventy-five percent of its income coming from government grants, could well serve as a model for the provision of a broad range of educational and informational services to meet human rights and human development needs using new distribution techniques.

◆   ◆   ◆

Thirty years before the label "knowledge economy" had become a fashionable political catch-cry, a television channel was set up in Canada's Ontario province with another very broad legislative mandate to provide high quality and distinctive educational programming for everyone. The *Ontario Educational Communications Authority Act 1970* (revised in 1980) formally required the channel:

"(a) to initiate, acquire, produce, distribute exhibit or otherwise deal in programs and materials in the educational and communications fields;

(b) to engage in research in those fields of activity consistent with the objects of the Authority under clause (a); and

(c) to discharge such other duties relating to educational broadcasting and communications as the Board considers to be incidental or conducive to the attainment of the objects mentioned in clauses (a) and (b)."

TVOntario (TVO) captures the spirit of this mandate in more everyday language as "providing Ontarians of all ages with programming that broadens understanding and responds to specific learning needs."

It pulls off this neat double act by scheduling some seventy percent of formal educational programmes during the day, with the balance made up of documentaries, current affairs and drama programmes and films, and then by reversing the ratios in prime time at night, when eighty percent of the schedule becomes broadly-based, while the balance is targeted at children, youth and distance learners.

Like Britain's Channel Four, it sees this broad-based prime time service as fulfilling the "informing and educating" responsibilities of a public service broadcaster, but in ways that offer innovation, and so a genuine alternative, to the rest of the market, whether public or private sector.

It describes this alternative schedule this way: "...award-winning science programs, point-of-view documentaries from Canada's best independent film makers, cultural programming focussing on local artists, the best drama and foreign films from around the world, and current affairs programs that provide thoughtful, in-depth coverage and discussions on the most important issues facing Ontarians."

It achieves this with a staff of about 400 and a budget in the region of $(U.S.) fifty million. About three-quarters of this comes from provincial and federal government grants; the rest from a variety of sources, including programme sales, annual subscriptions from more than 90,000 individual members, and a relatively small number of corporate sponsorships.

So TVO is, like Britain's Channel Four and Australia's SBS, both complementary and to a degree competitive with the state's original national public service broadcaster, in this case, Canada's CBC, as well as with America's PBS and a range of other public and private service choices available to most Canadians.

In such a competitive market viable audience shares are historically quite small, but TVO is able to claim that it's effective in its Canadian programming for children, capturing twenty-four percent of that target market as against sixteen percent achieved by a combination of the CBC, PBS and similar channels; and sixty percent by the commercial networks.

A trustee for the young

Many children's programmes carried by the commercial operators and sold internationally have of course long been recognised as little more than marketing vehicles for U.S.-made toys. And this advertising works: the percentage of toys sold in the U.S. that was directly linked to films and television rose from ten percent in 1984 to fifty percent in 1990, according to research by the American Psychological Association.

But TVO, like Japan's giant public broadcaster NHK, is a founder-member of Public Broadcasters International (PBI), whose value commitments include programming for children and acting as a trustee for the young. So the niche market of local content, public service programming for children, is a valid performance measure when it's reckoned that, by the time they're eighteen, children have spent more time watching television (14,000 hours) than they have in attending school classes (12,000 hours).

A 1999 report by the Royal Australasian College of Physicians, for example, said that children started watching television soon after they were born. Sydney children only four months old watched an average of forty-four minutes of television a day; twelve-month-old children about an hour a day; and thirty-month-old children were watching an average of eighty-four minutes. By the age of four, the average time had increased to more than two and a half hours a day. In that time a child will see about seventy-five advertisements, or more than 25,000 a year. The report focuses on giving advice to care-givers about how best to manage what spokesperson Dr Peter Watson described as the "social morbidities" of television, pointing out that it was only by the ages of thirteen or fourteen that children realised that what they see "is determined by what sells most, and not what is entirely accurate and true."

But trying to persuade parents to cut the current twenty-two or so viewing hours a week is only one approach, and, some would say an unrealistic goal, especially when the growing fascination with the small screen of the PC is thrown into the equation for this play-station generation.

Another option is for the state to intervene to influence the range and quality of local content programming available for children, whether distributed by the television or the PC screen, by setting up a body with an objective like TVOs.

By the turn of the century TVO was using a variety of media as complementary distribution systems of its services, with almost 500,000 people a week visiting its web-site and over 740,000 people a year logging-on to its e-mail services. It was able to claim, justifiably, that it was helping to integrate technology within the classroom: television programming, fax, phone, e-mail and web-sites.

The verdict of TVO's industry peers: more than 800 awards for its programmes, including the 1998 'Milia d'or' multi-media award, which it won in competition with trans-national giants like Disney and Sony.

SBS: "the most multicultural channel"

SBS Australia, financed eighty percent by government grants, could be a model for the deliberate use of broadcast communications to create a high-profile symbol of state-building (or re-building), so meeting democratic and political public policy objectives, while delivering both information and entertainment in a cost-effective way, and so also meeting social and cultural policy objectives.

◆   ◆   ◆

Ten years after TVOntario's different style of programming captured the interest of children and the wider public in Canada, the Special Broadcasting Service (SBS) began a different range of specialist television services in Australia. It was borne from impatience by Malcolm Fraser's Liberal-National (centre-right) coalition government with what it saw as the failure of both the public (ABC) and private sector television networks to reflect the transformation of Australia from a predominantly Anglo-Celtic (not Anglo-Saxon!) society into one of the most multi-cultural countries in the world.

This new ethnic and cultural profile followed a change in immigration policy after the Second World War. This opened the door to waves of immigrants, many non-English-speaking, from southern Europe, especially Italy, Greece and the former Yugoslavia, to add to the original northern European base with its substantial 19th century intake from Ireland as well as from Britain.

Today some thirty percent of all Australians reckon they have some Irish ancestry: in my time at the ABC Ireland's RTÉ sent a programme team to Sydney and later told me that even they were surprised by the strength of the Irish community they found there. But even by the mid-1970s the different mix of the Australian demographic cocktail was already quite evident from the people one saw on the streets and in the shops, and from the greater variety of restaurants. I made my first visit to study Melbourne radio developments in this era and was told then that it had the third highest Greek population of any city in the world, including those in Greece itself. So it was there, as well as in Sydney, that the SBS television service began in 1980, building on some early forays into multilingual radio provided by the ethnic radio pioneers, 2EA Sydney and 3EA Melbourne.

By the turn of the century, SBS-TV coverage had been extended to 17.5 million people, ninety percent of the Australian population, so that it's now a national broadcaster. While it was then achieving just over a four percent audience share of the five main city audiences, it was also being sampled by as many as six million Australians a week nationwide.

In a country whose population is now drawn from about 160 ethnic, cultural and linguistic groups, SBS television now broadcasts in more than sixty languages. Early evening prime time, though, is reserved for news, current affairs and sports programmes in English, the common language because it is the language of the state and, for SBS-TV, the most effective way to bridge its audience's diverse language groups. This strategy also reflects the evolution within Australia itself and of the SBS as an institution, from ethno-specific concerns in the earlier days to the cross-cultural remit of today: in many ways, a harder one to achieve.

A symbol of "new Australia"

SBS is now a firm symbol of a "new century Australia" whose people are rapidly becoming even more cosmopolitan. But it wasn't accepted so readily in the beginning. Then there were social and cultural concerns, as well as private sector industry anxieties. Kerry Packer, the owner of the Channel Nine network, was one who voiced his concern for Australia's future, fearing that ethnic television would become a divisive force in society. At the same time, the private sector seemed apprehensive that any new player, even one then limited to sponsorship revenues to add to its annual federal government grant, would somehow destabilise the market place; while for the ABC, it became a competitor for a share of federal government money.

But by then more than forty percent of Australians had either been born overseas or had at least one parent from overseas. Like the U.S., Australia, apart of course from the indigenous Aboriginal peoples, is a country of immigrants predominantly from the West, but with some from Asia as well.

No-one, therefore, should have been surprised that by the late 1970s a federal government should want to put down a high-profile marker on the ultimate direction of these evolving social and cultural changes by establishing SBS-TV.

The decision to set up what was to become the original radio-only SBS was announced in 1977; a regulation authorising the provision of multilingual television services, implicitly rather than explicitly to have a multicultural tone, was made in 1978; the recommendations of an Ethnic Television Review Panel were accepted in 1980, and later that same year, SBS-TV was on air.

However, the development of this aspect of communications policies was in some ways ahead of the development of a formal nationwide public policy on multi-culturalism, which crystallised on an all-party basis only during the 1980s after SBS-TV had arrived.

Only in 1982 did the Australian Council of Population and Ethnic Affairs summarise the principles of a multi-cultural society as "social cohesion; recognition of the validity of cultural identity (that is, cultural pluralism); equality of opportunity and access; and equal responsibility for, commitment to and participation in society." Only in 1987 did the Office of Multicultural Affairs publish *Preparing for the next century: the national agenda for a multi-cultural Australia;*

and only in 1988 did the House of Representatives pass a resolution re-affirming its own commitment to multiculturalism.

Meanwhile, SBS-TV, like SBS-Radio in 1978, and like RTÉ television in Ireland in 1960, had its statutory roots in radio-era, 1940s legislation—in this case, Australia's *Broadcasting Act 1942*. A new Part IIIA in a 1977 amending Act was used to set up the SBS, but as a later federal government discussion paper noted, this had a number of "…curious imbalances and gaps. There are some eighty lines describing the offices of the executive director and acting executive director, but hardly anything on what the SBS as a whole should be doing…the references to programs…are fleeting…Yet programs are the essential currency of any broadcaster."

"An instrument of social policy"

So the SBS was launched without any explicit statutory policy guidelines, leading inevitably to questions that focused on what it was there for, why and how its performance could be realistically assessed, either by the political financiers or by the public.

These questions were addressed by the Connor Report, which had looked at the place of broadcasting in the "new Australia" and which came out in 1985: as it turned out, in between the two key public policy papers on multiculturalism of 1982 and 1987. It saw broadcasting as having the potential to be "a vital instrument in the application of social policies," both because of its capacity to "reflect, shape and modify the attitude of the community to itself," and because it could provide "an important means of meeting the settlement and cultural needs of migrant communities."

When the decision to develop the SBS's current legislation was announced in 1989, it was able to be placed in the wider policy context of the government's *National agenda for a multi-cultural Australia*. So the *Special Broadcasting Service Act 1991*, amended in 1998, includes both a charter (s. 6) and a set of specific duties for its governing board (s. 10) (Appendix 3 (d) (iv)). Introducing the legislation in the Senate, the minister for industrial relations, Senator Cook, said that from then on SBS would be expected to "increase awareness of the contribution of a diversity of cultures to the continuing development of Australian society and to promote understanding and acceptance of that diversity."

The charter therefore begins by making it plain that SBS services are for all Australians and not just for recently-arrived immigrants, and that it's the job of the SBS to reflect the country's developing multi-cultural society to everyone.

This change of emphasis was quickly reflected by a change in the SBS logo, from "Bringing the world back home," to "Special programming for special people. Australians." Then it gives another sharper focus by formally identifying the communications needs of the indigenous Aboriginal and Torres Strait Islander communities, and joining them with the needs of ethnic communities, together forming Australia's multi-cultural society.

This charter provision fired the official starting gun for a broadening of the SBS's obligation to meet the special interests of minorities in tandem with its other mandate, to facilitate the sharing of cultures among all Australians. Like Britain's Channel Four, since 1982 one of the programme sources for SBS-TV, especially of "alternative" documentary and drama, the charter requires the SBS to reflect the changing nature of Australian society "by presenting many points of view and using innovative forms of expression."

So, not just another public forum but a complementary, different one.

The verdict of the people: surveys reported at the turn of the century showed eighty seven percent thought it important that SBS-TV provide an alternative to Australia's mainstream commercial channels, and seventy-six percent wanted it as an alternative to the ABC. In terms of the federal government's broader social and cultural policy framework, seventy-three percent said SBS-TV gives Australians a better understanding of immigrants, while sixty-eight percent said it gave them a greater degree of acceptance.

Summary: a cafeteria of policy choices

These three models are just some of the wide range of choices available to government ministers and their policy advisers, wanting either to review existing state-funded television services or planning to establish a new one as part of a multi-media corporation with statutory objectives more relevant to the 21st century.

They have the benefit of having been tried and tested for between twenty and thirty years. Each reflects a degree of government intervention in the market-place to achieve particular policy objectives. Each shows how the original theory was later slightly modified in the light of practical experience.

So the three models are valid examples of ways in which the political agenda can be broadened and how a variety of services can be provided at a relatively low cost with, say, a staff of 400 to 700, and with an operating budget of around $(U.S.) fifty million.

5

Conclusion: Globalisation won't go away

External and domestic interests

Governments can't afford to ignore the policy nexus between globalisation and, at least in the West's case, the need for the active protection and maintenance of liberal democracy at home.

It's in the *national* interest of countries in the West to maximise their influence at both the regional and global levels of international relations through this new quarter century of shifting power relativities. It's also in the *political* interest of their leaders that something's done to reinvigorate democracy at home, and to help all their people through the latest phases of ICT change.

Globalisation won't stop, or go away; like anything else, it needs to be managed. The new multi-media corporations have significant impacts at both the level of foreign policy and of domestic policy, and these need to be recognised and addressed by the governments of states. Ultimately, no one else can do so effectively.

Foreign policies: "the market will not suffice"

At the foreign policy level, governments are now beginning to recognise that the commercial interests of transnational multi-media corporations won't always match the public interests of their home state, or of organisational groupings of like-minded states. An obvious example is Rupert Murdoch's long-term strategy for his satellite television channels to gain media access to China's domestic market of over one billion people.

He angered China's leadership in 1993 by saying that satellite television and telecommunications posed an "unambiguous threat to totalitarian regimes everywhere." Ever since then he's worked hard to repair this damage to his company's

51

interests, starting by dropping BBC world service television news from his Asian satellite broadcaster Star TV in 1994 after it had shown a documentary critical of Mao Tse-tung.

That same year, his HarperCollins publishing house published a biography, seen by critics as inevitably one-sided, of Chinese leader Deng Xiaping, written by his daughter, Deng Rong. Four years later, ironically, Murdoch told Harper-Collins *not* to publish another book: this one, the memoirs of Hong Kong's last British governor, Chris Patten. He had angered China by moving to democratise Hong Kong's political system in the closing years of Britain's one hundred-year responsibility, and just before Hong Kong's return to China in 1997.

By the end of the 20th century Murdoch's strategy seemed to be paying off for his business. He met the then President Jiang Zemin, who praised his efforts "in presenting China objectively." By early the following year, Murdoch was able to tell a Singapore forum on media prospects for the 21st century that News Corp was making "very significant progress" in its key target markets of China, Taiwan and India. During 1999, he sparked another wave of speculation about the future control of his media empire when he married a Chinese, Yale-educated, former employee, Wendi Deng, speculation that Murdoch brushed aside in a rare interview, in the U.S. magazine *Vanity Fair*.

However, what seems a sensible and potentially successful policy strategy from News Corp's perspective may not seem so good when looked at through a different lens.

Murdoch's decision on the Patten book angered U.S. politicians and U.S. campaigners for human rights in China. Murdoch irritated them further with his 1999 description of Tibet's exiled Dalai Lama as "a very political monk in Gucci shoes," while his earlier decision to drop BBC television news broadcasts was seen at least by some as demonstrating a failure of the market.

One who takes this view is Joseph Nye, who has used the label "soft power" to describe what he sees as a new and more effective form of power, one based on achieving desired outcomes through attraction rather then coercion.

His argument is that America holds, and in his view will continue to hold for at least a decade, a comparative advantage in its ability to collect, process, act upon and disseminate information, a key element of "soft power." But, he argues, this is still not being widely acknowledged by some in the U.S. Congress. The Voice of America, he points out, broadcasts in forty-eight languages and has an audience tens of millions greater than the U.S. private sector transnational company CNN, which broadcasts only in English. But VOA's role in China, he says, in fact "illustrates the problem of market failure." It became the leading source of news for educated Chinese not as a result of a U.S. government or VOA policy, but largely by default, because of Murdoch's commercially-motivated decision to end the BBC transmissions.

For the implementation of foreign policy objectives, Nye concludes, the market "will not suffice."

Domestic policies: the market still won't suffice

Nor will the market suffice in meeting any state's domestic democratic, political, social or cultural policy objectives, largely because it isn't its job to do so. The increasing availability of television channels gives governments the soft option of suggesting to their citizens that this choice, mainly a consumer service, is all they need.

But more channels don't necessarily mean more real choices. Even more importantly, their entertainment focus and ratings-driven formats don't and won't fill a role that should be accepted as justification for intervention in the market-place by the state itself, in fulfilment of its human rights obligations towards its people as citizens.

So I don't view the latest technical change, digitalisation, allowing up to 500 channels for some people in some cities of some states, with much enthusiasm. This is because the cost of programme production of even a reasonable quality is always rising. Even with a greater number of international co-productions, the range and certainly the quality of product, simply isn't there to fill the channels and the combined time available on all their schedules.

For most states there will almost certainly have to be a further increase in the levels of imported programmes, which as we've seen is already high in many countries because it is of course always much cheaper to import someone else's programmes at marginal cost than to make your own.

So the West as a whole, and particularly the smaller states with fewer resources, tighter economic margins and so greater pressure on public sector managers, will need even more determination and political willpower if they are to have any chance of redressing this increasing imbalance.

That will mean a set of policies integrating communications under the umbrella of national cultural identity policies and recognising the central importance of what I argue is a newly-important, transcendental role for public service television: as a consciously-recognised instrument of democratic process affecting one hundred percent of people, not just the twenty percent or so interested in national cultural identity. It will then mean governments allowing for effective implementation of this as a strategic priority by providing a clear statutory framework and a secure financing base, not with an unfinanced or insufficiently financed mandate, as so often happens.

And, whether or not it fits the ideological philosophies of free market governments, that will also mean a degree of broadcasting regulation or, in New Zealand's case, where there's been virtually no regulation at all since the mid-1980s, of re-regulation combined with re-structuring.

State responses: "the public interest"

It's about time that we got back to basics over what is meant by the phrase "the public interest."

During the dominance of free market thinking in the last twenty years, a generation, efforts have been made by ruling elites to redefine it so that we feel that "the interests of the public" are met because, the argument runs, the public is the ultimate beneficiary of the market. That ultimate benefit, the "trickle down" theory, is of course now being increasingly questioned both from an economic and social perspective, as imbalances between and within states become wider instead of narrower.

The ideological pendulum shows signs of swinging back a little, the normal correction likely to any set of policies over a period of time, but still, at this stage, within an overall free market framework. Some Western leaders have argued that they accept a market economy but not a market society; in other words, they aim to restore some lost balances to society, but without abandoning the drive to freer markets.

In my context of the interplay between the global free market, the state and democracy in terms of communications policies, and specifically, the use of television as a medium, I think it's time for the state to redress this imbalance. Governments need to go back to the idea of the public interest as being met by government policies and actions, which have as their over-riding objective the welfare of the people through a selective but deliberate intervention in the market place.

In communications policy terms, that surely must mean policies and actions that make available to every citizen both the information and the cultural resources to allow each of us the chance to participate more effectively in the democratic and political process and to debate ways of achieving or maintaining social cohesion, based on a widely-accepted statement of national cultural identity.

The American lawyer Price, quoted earlier, takes a tough line on this: if the state can't, or by implication won't, satisfactorily generate, sustain, or encourage "narratives to communal well-being" and remain true to democratic values, then he says, "the question becomes one of state survival."

I'm not sure I would go quite as far as that, but I would agree with another of his judgements, that the case for a television service with obligations *other than to the market* "will ultimately rest on the need for reinforcement of the idea of community, the strengthening of democratic values, and the idea of the state."

That case can best be met by a multi-media public corporation with a primary role as a programme provider, using all available means of transmission, television, radio, print and on-line, to distribute its services free of charge to everyone, but without necessarily owning the means of transmission.

There will be a cost to the nation in that, but, after all, there is also a price to pay for tending the flame of democracy.

Sources

Introduction:

Nye, Joseph S.: *Bound to lead: the changing nature of American power, 1991*

Chapter 1:

Harris Poll*: Alienation index, 1999*
Heyward A.: *The Seven deadly sins of television news* in: *Television Quarterly, 1997*
Huntington, Samuel P.: *The clash of civilisations and the remaking of world order, 1996; The lonely superpower, 1999*
Price, Monroe E.: *Television, the public sphere and national identity, 1995*
Revel, Jean-Francois: *Democracy against itself, 1993*
U.S. Federal Election Commission: *Presidential elections, 1932–2000*
UNESCO: *World communication and information report, 1999–2000, 1999*
Wattenberg, P.: *The crisis of electoral politics, 1997*
Wessberg, A.: *Public service broadcasting* in: UNESCO (ibid.)

Chapter 2:

United States:
U.S. government: *Public Broadcasting Act, 1967*
Juneau, P.: *Small nations, big neighbour, 1993*
Price: ibid
Tracey, M.: *The United States, PBS and the limitations of a mainstream alternative* in: *Public Broadcasting for the 21st century, 1995*

Britain:
British Broadcasting Corporation: *Annual Report, 1999*
BBC Director-General Dyke, G.: *My vision for the BBC* (in *The Spectator*, 20 November, 1999)

Canada:

Canadian government: *Canadian Broadcasting Act, 1991*

CRTC: *From vision to results at the CRTC, 1997*

Ostry, B.: *Public television must go global,* in *Ottawa Citizen, 1991*

Raboy, M.: *Canada: the hybridisation of Canadian Broadcasting,* in *Public Broadcasting for the 20th century, 1995*

Australia:

Australian Federal government: *Dix Report (five volumes), 1981; Australian Broadcasting Corporation Act, 1983; Special Broadcasting Services Act, 1991/1998; Mansfield Report: The challenge of a better ABC 1997*

Ireland:

Brown, Terence: *Ireland: a social and cultural history. 1922–1985, 1985*

The Economic and Social Research Institute *Medium-term review, 1997–2003, 1997*

Irish government: legislation, especially the *Wireless and Telegraphy Act, 1926; Broadcasting Authority Act,1960; Broadcasting Authority (Amendment) Act, 1976; Radio and Television Act, 1988; Broadcasting Act, 1990; EC (Television Broadcasting) Regulations, 1991; Broadcasting Authority (Amendment) Act, 1993; Broadcasting Act 2001; Broadcasting (Funding) Bill, 2003.*

Irish government: Green Paper *Active or passive? Broadcasting in the future tense, 1995*

RTÉ: *Response to the government's Green Paper on broadcasting (1995); Forum on Broadcasting, 2002.*

RTÉ: *Annual reports*

Truetzschler, W: in: *The Media in Europe, 2004.*

New Zealand:

Adam, K. (chairman): *The broadcasting future of New Zealand, 1973*

Gregory, R.J.: *Politics and broadcasting: before and beyond the NZBC, 1985*

Henderson, D.: *The changing fortunes of economic liberalism: yesterday, today and tomorrow, 1998*

Ministry of Cultural Affairs: *Government's role in the public sector: a survey of the issues, 1998*

New Zealand government: *State-Owned Enterprises Act, 1986/1995; Broadcasting Act, 1989/1998; Television New Zealand Act, 2003*

Ord Minnett: *Scoping TVNZ, 1997*

Spicer, Powell, Emanuel: *The remaking of Television New Zealand, 1984–1992, 1996*
Stevenson, J. (chairman*): Officials committee on broadcasting, 1988*
Television New Zealand: *Annual reports and Statements of Intent*

United Nations:
UNESCO: *'World Communications Report' (1989, 1997 and 1999)*

Chapter 3:

Broadcasting Research Unit: *The public service idea in British broadcasting—main principles 1986*
Council of Europe: *Convention for the protection of human rights and fundamental freedom, 1950*
European Commission*: The digital age: European audiovisual policy, 1998*
European Union: *Fourth ministerial conference on mass media policy, 1994*
European Union*: European Parliament and Council Directive 97/36/EC, amending 89/552/EEC—Television without frontiers, 1997*
Council of Europe: *Recommendation R (99) 1 on measures to promote media pluralism, 1999*
Public Broadcasters International: *Conference communiqué, (Toronto, Canada, November, 1991).*
UN: *Human Rights Declaration, 1948; International covenant on civil and political rights, 1966*
UNESCO: *Mass media declaration (1978; amended 1989)*
UNESCO: *World Communication Reports* (ibid)
UNESCO/EC: *Cultural programmes on European public television channels, 1998*

Chapter 4:

Britain: Channel Four

Channel Four: *Statement of Programme Policy, 1998*
Channel Four: *Report and financial statements, 1998, 1999*
Independent Television Commission: *Revised Channel Four licence, (23 February, 1998)*

Independent Television Commission: Channel Four performance review, 1998, (in *ITC annual report and accounts: 1998*), 1999
Isaacs, J.: *We were all one of us to him* (in *The Spectator, 17 July, 1999*

Canada: TVOntario

Government of Ontario: *Ontario Educational and Communications Authority Act 1970/1980: 1982*
Open Learning Agency: *Vision and mission statements, 1998*
Royal Australasian College of Physicians: *Getting in the picture: a parent's and carer's guide for the better use of television for children, 1999*
TVOntario: *Facts and figures 1997–98, 1999;* various educational and programming services leaflets

Australia: SBS

Office of Multicultural Affairs: *Preparing for the next century: the national agenda for a multicultural Australia, 1987*
Committee of Review of the SBS (the *Connor Report*): *Serving multicultural Australia: the role of broadcasting, 1985*
Commonwealth Parliamentary Debates (House of Representatives): *Resolution on multi-culturalism, 17 March, 1988*
Department of Transport and Communications: *Review of national broadcasting policy: discussion paper—Special Broadcasting Service, 1988*
O'Regan, T. (with Kolar-Penov, D): *SBS-TV: a television service* in: *Australian television culture, 1993*
Special Broadcasting Service: *Corporate plan 1996–1999: outcomes report for 1998–9, 1999*
Special Broadcasting Service: *Television audiences, 1998, 1999*

Chapter 5:

Nye, J.: *Bound to lead: the changing nature of American power, 1991*
Nye and Owens, William A.: *America's information edge* (in *Foreign Affairs, March/April, 1996*)
Price, ibid

Bibliography

Adam, K. (chairman): *The broadcasting future of New Zealand, 1973*
Australian Federal Government: *Dix Report 1981; Mansfield Report, 1997*
Broadcasting Research Unit: *The public service idea in British broadcasting—main principles, 1986*
Brown, Terence: *Ireland: a social and cultural history 1922–1985 (1985)*
Chapman, R. (chairman): *Broadcasting and telecommunications in New Zealand: report of the Royal Commission of inquiry, 1986*
Committee of Review of the SBS (the Connor Report): *Serving multicultural Australia: the role of broadcasting, 1985*
Curran, C. J.: *A seamless robe: broadcasting philosophy and practice, 1979*
Department of Internal Affairs (NZ): *The New Zealand government and national identity, 1996*
Department of Transport and Communications (Australia): *Review of national broadcasting policy: discussion paper—Special Broadcasting Service 1988*
Easton, B.: *The commercialisation of New Zealand, 1997*
European Commission: *The digital age: European audiovisual policy 1998*
Gibbons, Luke: *Transformations in Irish culture, 1986*
Graham, Brian: *In search of Ireland, 1997*
Gregory, R.J.: *Politics and broadcasting: before and beyond the NZBC, 1985*
Harland, B.: *On our own: New Zealand in an emerging tripolar world, 1992*
Huntington, Samuel P.: *The clash of civilisations and the remaking of world order 1996; The lonely superpower, 1999*
Irish government: Green Paper *Active or passive? Broadcasting in the future tense, 1995*
Juneau, P.: *Small nations, big neighbour, 1993*
Kiber, Damien (ed): *Media in Ireland—the search for diversity, 1997*
McLoone, Martin (ed): *Culture identity and broadcasting in Ireland, 1991*
Ministry of Cultural Affairs (NZ): *Government's role in the public sector: a survey of the issues, 1998*
New Zealand On Air (NZOA): *Local content and diversity: television in ten countries, 1999; Our faces, our voices, ourselves, 1997; Local content and diversity: television in ten countries, 1999*

Nye, J.: *Bound to lead: the changing nature of American power 1991; The paradox of American power: why the world's only superpower can't go it alone, 2003*

Nye and Owens, William A.: *America's information edge* (in: *Foreign Affairs*, March/April, 1996)

Office of Multicultural Affairs (Australia): *Preparing for the next century: the national agenda for a multicultural Australia, 1987*

Ord, Minnett: Scoping TVNZ, 1997

O'Regan, T. (with Kolar-Penov, D): *SBS-TV: a television service* in: *Australian television culture, 1993*

O'Toole, Fintan: *The lie of the land: Irish identities, 1998*

Peacock, A. (chairman): *Report of the committee on financing the BBC, 1986*

Price, Monroe E.: *Television, the public sphere and national identity, 1995*

Raboy, M. and others: *Public Broadcasting for the 20th century, 1995*

Revel, Jean-Francois: *Democracy against itself, 1993*

RTÉ: *Response to the government's Green Paper on broadcasting, 1995*

Savage, Robert J.: *Irish television—the political and social origins, 1996*

The Economic and Social Research Institute (Ireland): *Medium-term review. 1997–2003, 1997*

Waters, John: *An intelligent person's guide to modern Ireland, 1997*

APPENDIX

International, regional and national policy models

1. INTERNATIONAL

(a) *UN Human Rights Declaration (1948): Article 19:*

"Everyone has the right to freedom of opinion and expression; this right includes freedom to hold opinions without interference and to seek, receive and impart information and ideas through any media and regardless of frontiers."

(b) *International Covenant on Civil and Political Rights (1966): Article 19:*

"Everyone shall have the right to freedom of expression; this right shall include freedom to seek, receive and impart information and ideas of all kinds, regardless of frontiers, either orally, in writing or in print, in the form of art, or through any other media of his (sic) choice."

(c) *UNESCO Mass Media Declaration (1978)*

"Declaration on fundamental principles concerning the contribution of the mass media to strengthening peace and international understanding, to the promotion of human rights and to countering racialism, apartheid and incitement to war.
1. Preamble
The General Conference—
Recalling that by virtue of its Constitution the purpose of UNESCO is to 'contribute to peace and security by promoting collaboration among the nations through education, science and culture in order to further universal respect for justice, for the rule of law and for the human rights and fundamental freedoms'

(Art. I, 1), and that to realise this purpose the organisation will strive 'to promote the free flow of ideas by word and image' (Art, I, 2)...

Recalling the purposes and principles of the United Nations, as specified in its Charter.

Recalling the Universal Declaration of Human Rights, adopted by the General Assembly of the United Nations in 1948 and particularly Article 19 thereof...and the International Covenant on Civil and Political Rights, adopted by the General Assembly of the United Nations in 1966, Article 19 of which proclaims the same principles...

Proclaims on this twenty-eighth day of November 1978 this declaration...

Article 1—

The strengthening of peace and international understanding, the promotion of human rights and the countering of racialism...demand a free flow and a wider and better balanced dissemination of information. To this end, the mass media have a leading contribution to make. This contribution will be the more effective to the extent that the information reflects the different aspects of the subject dealt with.

Article 2—

(i) The exercise of freedom of opinion, expression and information, recognised as an integral part of human rights and fundamental freedoms, is a vital factor in the strengthening of peace and international understanding.

(ii) Access by the public to information should be guaranteed by the diversity of the sources and means of information available to it, thus enabling each individual to check the accuracy of facts and to appraise events objectively. To this end, journalists must have freedom to report and the fullest possible facilities of access to information. Similarly, it is important that the mass media be responsive to concerns of peoples and individuals, thus promoting the participation of the public in the elaboration of information...

Article 3—

(ii) In encountering...violations of human rights which are inter alia spawned by prejudice and ignorance, the mass media, by disseminating information on the aims, aspirations, cultures and needs of all peoples, contribute to eliminate ignorance and misunderstanding between peoples, to make nationals of a country sensitive to the needs and desires of others...

Article 10—

(i) With due respect for constitutional provisions designed to guarantee freedom of information and for the applicable international instruments and agreements, it is indispensable to create and maintain throughout the world the conditions

which make it possible for the organisations and persons professionally involved in the dissemination of information to achieve the objectives of this Declaration. (ii) It is important that a free flow and wider and better balanced dissemination of information be encouraged...
Article 11—
For this declaration to be fully effective it is necessary, with due respect for the legislative and administrative provisions and the other obligations of member states, to guarantee the existence of favourable conditions for the operation of the mass media, in conformity with the provisions of the Universal Declaration of Human Rights and with the corresponding principles proclaimed in the International Covenant on Civil and Political Rights adopted by the General Assembly of the United Nations in 1966."

(d) Public Broadcasters International (PBI) mission statement (1991)

"To serve the varied needs, tastes, and interests of mass and minority audiences, while upholding the integrity of diverse cultures and languages;

- To provide quality programming for children and adults that informs, educates, entertains, and advances social equity;

- To maintain editorial integrity and operational independence from political, ideological, and economic intervention;

- To foster the development of distinctive and creative programming that challenges our audiences;

- To enrich and strengthen the cultural, social, and economic fabrics of the communities we serve;

- To deepen national and international mutual understanding of peoples and their social, ecological, economic, political, cultural, and technological environments;

- To help people understand the significance of global changes to their lives and to their communities;

- To actively involve viewers and listeners in establishing programming and service directions;

- To use new and existing technologies to extend the range and effectiveness of our services."

2. REGIONAL

(a) *Fourth European Ministerial Conference on Mass Media Policy (1994):*

Resolution No. 1: The future of public service broadcasting
"The Ministers of the States...
Acknowledging that public service broadcasting, both radio and television, support the values underlying the political, legal and social structures of democratic societies, and in particular respect for human rights, culture and political pluralism;
Stressing the importance of public service broadcasting for democratic societies;
Recognising therefore the need to guarantee the permanence of stability of public service broadcasting so as to allow it to continue to operate in the service of the public;
Underlining the vital function of public service broadcasting as an essential factor of pluralistic communication accessible to everyone;
Recalling the importance of radio and stressing its great potential for the development of democratic societies, particularly at the regional and local levels;
1. General principles
Affirm their commitment to maintain and develop a strong public service broadcasting system in an environment characterised by an increasingly competitive offer of programme services and rapid technological change...
Undertake to guarantee at least one comprehensive wide-range programme service comprising information, education, culture and entertainment which is accessible to all members of the public, while acknowledging that public service broadcasters must also be permitted to provide, where appropriate, additional programme services such as thematic services;
Undertake to define clearly...the role, missions and responsibilities of public service broadcasters and to ensure their editorial independence against political and economic interference;
Undertake to guarantee public service broadcasters secure and appropriate means necessary for the fulfilment of their missions;
Agree to implement these commitments in accordance with the following framework:
2. Policy framework for public service broadcasting
Public Service Requirements
Participating States agree that public service broadcasters...must have principally the following missions:

(i) To provide, through their programming, a reference point for all members of the public and a factor for social cohesion and integration of all individuals, groups and communities. In particular, they must reject any cultural, sexual, religious or racial discrimination and any form of social segregation;

(ii) To provide a forum for public discussion in which as broad a spectrum as possible of views and opinions can be expressed;

(iii) To broadcast impartial and independent news, information and comment;

(iv) To develop pluralistic, innovatory and varied programming which meets high ethical and quality standards and not to sacrifice the pursuit of quality to market forces;

(v) To develop and structure programme schedules and services of interest to a wide public while being attentive to the needs of minority groups;

(vi) To reflect the different philosophical ideas and religious beliefs in society, with the aim of strengthening mutual understanding and tolerance and promoting community relations in pluriethnic and multicultural societies;

(vii) To contribute actively through their programming to a greater appreciation and dissemination of the diversity of national and European cultural heritage;

(viii) To ensure that the programmes offered contain a significant proportion of original productions, especially feature films, drama and other creative works, and to have regard to the need to use independent producers and co-operate with the cinema sector; and

(ix) To extend the choice available to viewers and listeners by also offering programme services which are not normally provided by commercial broadcasters.'

Funding

Participating states undertake to maintain and, where necessary, establish an appropriate and secure funding framework which guarantees public service broadcasters the means necessary to accomplish their missions…

The level of licence fee or public subsidy should be projected over a sufficient period of time so as to allow public service broadcasters to engage in long term planning.

Economic Practices

Participating states should endeavour to ensure that economic practices such as the concentration of media ownership, the acquisition of exclusive rights and the control over distribution systems such as conditional access techniques, do not prejudice the vital contribution public service broadcasters have to make pluralism and the right of the public to receive information.

Independence and Accountability
Participating states undertake to guarantee the independence of public service broadcasters against political and economic interference...
Public service broadcasters must be directly accountable to the public. To that end, public service broadcasters should regularly publish information on their activities and develop procedures for allowing viewers and listeners to comment on the way in which they carry out their missions."

(b) *Television without frontiers European Parliament/Council of Europe Directives (1989/1997):*

Directive 97/36/EC amending directive 89/552/EEC on the co-ordination of certain provisions concerning television broadcasting activities.
"Each Member State may take measures in accordance with Community Law to ensure that broadcasters under its jurisdiction do not broadcast on an exclusive basis events which are regarded by that Member State as being of major importance for society in such a way as to deprive a substantial proportion of the public in that Member State of the possibility of following such events via live coverage or deferred coverage on free television. If it does so, the Member State concerned shall draw up a list of designated events, national or non-national, which it considers to be of major importance for society. It shall do so in a clear and transparent manner in due and effective time. In so doing the Member State concerned shall also determine whether these events should be available via whole or partial live coverage, or where necessary or appropriate for objective reasons in the public interest, whole or partial deferred coverage."

(c) *Council of Europe: Recommendation No. R (99) 1 on Measures to promote Media Pluralism (1999):*

"The Committee of Ministers...Stressing the importance for individuals to have access to pluralistic media content, in particular as regards information;
Stressing also that the media, and in particular the public service broadcasting sector, should enable different groups and interests in society—including linguistic, social, economic, cultural or political minorities—to express themselves;
Noting that the existence of a multiplicity of autonomous and independent media outlets at the national, regional and local levels generally enhances pluralism and democracy...

Stressing that States should promote political and cultural pluralism by developing their media policy in line with Article 10 of the European Convention on Human Rights...

Noting...that the establishment of dominant positions and the development of media concentrations might be furthered by the technological convergence between the broadcasting, telecommunications and computer sectors...

Recommends that the government of the member States:

(i) examine the measures contained in the appendix to this recommendation and consider the inclusion of these in their domestic law or practice where appropriate, with a view to promoting media pluralism;

(ii) evaluate on a regular basis the effectiveness of their existing measures to promote pluralism and/or anti-concentration mechanisms and examine the possible need to revise them in the light of economic and technological developments in the media field.

Appendix to Recommendation No. R (99) 1

Measures to promote media pluralism

I. Regulation of ownership: broadcasting and the press

Member States should consider the introduction of legislation designed to prevent or counteract concentrations that might endanger media pluralism at the national, regional or local levels. Member States should examine the possibility of defining thresholds—in their law or authorisation, licensing or similar procedures—to limit the influence which a single commercial company or group may have in one or more media sectors. Such thresholds may for example take the form of a maximum audience share or be based on the revenue/turnover of commercial media companies. Capital share limits in commercial media enterprises may also be considered. If thresholds are introduced, member States should take into consideration the size of the media market and the level of resources available in it. Companies which have reached the permissible thresholds in a relevant market should not be awarded additional broadcasting licences for that market.

Over and above these measures, national bodies responsible for awarding licences to private broadcasters should pay particular attention to the promotion of media pluralism in the discharge of their mission.

Member States may consider the possibility of creating specific media authorities invested with powers to act against mergers or other concentration operations that threaten media pluralism or investing regulatory bodies for the broadcasting sector with such powers. In the event member States would not consider this appropriate, the general competition authorities should pay particular attention to media pluralism when reviewing mergers or other concentration operations in the media sector.

Member States should consider the adoption of specific measures where vertical integration—that is, the control of key elements of production, broadcasting, distribution and related activities by a single company or group—may be detrimental to pluralism...

III Media content
1. General principle
Member States should consider possible measures to ensure that a variety of media content reflecting different political and cultural views is made available to the public, bearing in mind the importance of guaranteeing the editorial independence of the media and the value which measures adopted on a voluntary basis by the media themselves may also have.

2. Broadcasting sector
Member states should consider, where appropriate and practicable, introducing measures to promote the production and broadcasting of diverse content by broadcasting organisations. Such measures could for instance be to require in broadcasting licences that a certain volume of original programmes, in particular as regards news and current affairs, is produced or commissioned by broadcasters. Furthermore, under certain circumstances, such as the exercise of a dominant position by a broadcaster in a particular area, member States could foresee "frequency sharing" arrangements so as to provide access to the airways for other broadcasters.

Member States should examine the introduction of rules aimed at preserving a pluralistic local radio and television landscape, ensuring in particular that networking, understood as the centralised provision of programmes and related services, does not endanger pluralism...

V. Public services broadcasting
Member States should maintain public service broadcasting and allow it to develop in order to make use of the possibilities offered by the new communication technologies and services. Member States should examine ways of developing forms of consultation of the public by public service broadcasting organisations, which may include the creation of advisory programme committees, so as to reflect in their programming policy the needs and requirements of the different groups in society...

With the prospect of digitisation, member States should consider maintaining "must carry" rules for cable networks. Similar rules could be envisaged, where necessary, for other distribution means and delivery platforms.

VI. Support measures for the media

Member States could consider the possibility of introducing, with a view to enhancing media pluralism and diversity, direct or indirect financial support schemes for both the print and broadcast media, in particular at the regional and local levels. Subsidies for media entities printing or broadcasting in a minority language could also be considered.'

3. NATIONAL

(a) The United States

(i) *The US Bill of Rights: Amendment 1 (1791):*
"Freedom of religion, speech and the press; rights of assembly and petition
Articles in addition to, and amendment of, the Constitution of the United States of America, proposed by Congress, and ratified by the several states, pursuant to the fifth article of the original constitution.

Congress shall make no law respecting an establishment of religion, or prohibiting the free exercise thereof; or abridging the freedom of speech, or of the press, or the right of the people peaceably to assemble, and to petition the Government for a redress of grievances."

(ii) *Public Broadcasting Act (1967)*

"Sec 396 Congressional Declaration of Policy
(a) The Congress hereby finds and declares:
(i) that it is in the public interest to encourage the growth and development of non-commercial educational radio and television broadcasting, including the use of such media for instructional purposes;
(ii) that expansion and development of non-commercial educational radio and television broadcasting and of diversity of its programming depend on freedom, imagination, and initiative on both the local and national levels;
(iii) that the encouragement and support of non-commercial educational radio and television broadcasting, while matters of importance for private and local

development, are also of appropriate and important concern to the Federal Government;

(iv) that it furthers the general welfare to encourage non-commercial educational radio and television broadcast programming which will be responsive to the interests of people both in particular localities and throughout the United States, and which will constitute an expression of diversity and excellence;

(v) that it is necessary and appropriate for the Federal Government to complement, assist, and support a national policy that will most effectively make non-commercial educational radio and television service available to all the citizens of the United States;

(vi) that a private corporation should be created to facilitate the development of educational radio and television broadcasting and to afford maximum protection to such broadcasting from extraneous interference and control."

(b) Britain

(i) *BBC Royal Charter—Introduction (1926–2006)*

"Elizabeth the Second by the Grace of God of the United Kingdom of Great Britain and Northern Ireland and of Our other Realms and Territories Queen, Head of the Commonwealth Defender of the Faith:

To all to whom these presents shall come, greeting!

Whereas on the twentieth day of December in the year of our Lord one thousand nine hundred and twenty-six by Letters made Patent under the Great Seal, Our Royal Predecessor His Majesty King George the Fifth granted unto the British Broadcasting Corporation (hereinafter called "the Corporation") a Charter of Incorporation.

And whereas on divers dates by Letters made Patent under the Great Seal, further Charters of Incorporation and Supplemental Charters have been granted unto the Corporation, the last such Charter having been granted to the Corporation on the seventh day of July One thousand nine hundred and eighty-one ("the Existing Charter").

And whereas the period of incorporation of the Corporation under the Existing Charter will expire on the thirty-first day of December One thousand nine hundred and ninety-six and it has been represented unto Us by Our right trusty and well beloved Counsellor Virginia Bottomley Our Secretary of State for National Heritage, that it is expedient that the Corporation should be continued for the period ending on the thirty-first day of December two thousand and six.

And whereas in view of the widespread interest which is taken by Our Peoples in broadcasting services and of the great value of such services as means of disseminating information, education and entertainment, We believe it to be in the interests of Our Peoples in Our United Kingdom and elsewhere within the Commonwealth that there should be an independent corporation which should continue to provide broadcasting services and should be permitted to provide other audio-visual services pursuant to such licences in that behalf as Our Secretary of State for Trade and Industry and such agreements in that behalf as Our Secretary of State may from time to time grant to and make with the Corporation.
Now know ye that We by Our Prerogative Royal and of Our especial grace, certain knowledge and mere motion do by this Our Charter for Us, Our Heirs and Successors will, ordain and declare as follows..."

(ii) *BBC licence and agreement—extracts (1996–2006)*

"Agreement between HM Secretary of State for National Heritage and the British Broadcasting Corporation—Treasury Minute (1995):

'...3. PROGRAMME CONTENT.
3.1 Without prejudice to the generality of clause 5, the Corporation undertakes to provide and keep under review the Home Services with a view to the maintenance of high general standards in all respects (and in particular in respect of their content, quality and editorial integrity) and to their offering a wide range of subject matter (having regard both to the programmes as a whole and also to the days of the week on which, and the times of the day at which, the programmes are shown) meeting the needs and interests of audiences, in accordance with the requirements specified in sub clause 3.2.

3.2 The requirements referred to in sub clause 3.1 are that the Home Services:

(a) are provided as a public service for disseminating information, education and entertainment.
(b) stimulate, support and reflect, in drama, comedy, music and the visual and performing arts, the diversity of cultural activity in the United Kingdom.
(c) contain comprehensive, authoritative and impartial coverage of news and current affairs in the United Kingdom and throughout the world to support fair and informed debate at local, regional and national levels.
(d) provide wide-ranging coverage of sporting and other leisure interests.

(e) contain programmes of an educational nature (including special factual, religious and social issues programmes as well as formal education and vocational training programmes).

(f) include a high standard of original programmes for children and young people.

(g) contain programmes which reflect the lives and concerns of both local and national audiences.

(h) contain a reasonable proportion and range of programmes for national audiences made in Northern Ireland, Scotland, Wales and in the English regions outside London and the South East.

3.3 The Corporation shall transmit an impartial account day by day prepared by professional reporters of the proceedings in both Houses of Parliament.

4. OBJECTIVES FOR THE HOME SERVICES
The Corporation shall:

4.1 publish objectives concerning the Home Services for inclusion in the Annual Report to be laid before Parliament pursuant to Article 18 of the Royal Charter.

4.2 publish and make available to all holders of television licences (within the meaning of section 1 of the Wireless Telegraphy Act 1949) an annual Statement of Promises to Audiences describing its services, standards and objectives.

4.3 undertake an appropriate process of public consultation prior to making any material change to the nature of the Home Services provided always that such consultation shall not require the BBC to disclose commercially sensitive matters relating to programme services.

4.4 report in reasonable detail on the performance of the Corporation in the Annual Report…"

(iii) *Independent Television Commission (ITC): Annual Report and Accounts: Conditions relating to the provision and content of the Channel Four service (1998):*

"General Matters:

1. The Channel 4 Service shall be provided as a public service for disseminating information, education and entertainment.

2. Channel 4 programmes shall contain a suitable proportion of matter calculated to appeal to tastes and interests not generally catered for by (the commercial) Channel 3.

3. Innovation and experiment in the form and content of Channel 4 programmes shall be encouraged.

4. The Channel 4 service shall be given a distinctive character of its own.

High General Standard:

5. Channel 4 programmes shall maintain a high general standard in all respects (and, in particular, in respect of their content and quality).

Diversity:

6. Channel 4 programmes shall maintain a wide range in their subject matter, having regard both to the programmes as a whole and also to the days of the week on which, and the times of the day at which, the programmes are broadcast. The peak-time schedule will incorporate programmes from a wide range of programme categories, including news, current affairs, education, religion and multicultural...

Educational Programmes

7....not less than seven hours per week of Channel 4 programmes, in addition to...schools programmes, shall be programmes of an educational nature.

News

8. In addition to any news service at breakfast time, not less than four hours per week of news programmes which are of high quality shall be included in the Channel 4 service. Such news programme shall be accurate, impartial, authoritative and comprehensive, in terms both of geography and subject matter, and live coverage of important, fast-moving events shall be provided, with news flashes outside regular bulletins as appropriate.

Current Affairs

9. Not less than four hours per week of current affairs programmes which are of high quality shall be included in the Channel 4 service.

Programming of European Origin

10. The majority of the transmission time on the Channel 4 service (excluding the time reserved to news, sports, events, games, advertising and teletext services) in each calendar year of the licence period shall be devoted to programming of European origin.

Independent Productions

11. In each year not less than 25 per cent...of the total amount of time allocated to the broadcasting of qualifying programmes in the Channel 4 service is allocated to the broadcasting of a range and diversity of independent productions...

Original Productions and Commissions

12. From 1999 at least 60 per cent by time of the programmes included in the licensed service in each calendar year shall be originally produced or

commissioned for Channel 4. The requirement for peak-time is 70 per cent.
Production Outside London
13. The Corporation shall use its best endeavours to ensure that in 2002 and
any subsequent calendar year at least 30 per cent of its programme budget is
allocated to the production of programmes by companies based outside London.
Repeats
14. The Corporation shall ensure that from 1999 no more than 40 per cent
of programmes transmitted in any calendar year have been previously shown
in the same or substantially the same form on Channel 4. The maximum for
peak-time is 20 per cent..."

(c) Canada

(i) *Broadcasting Act (1991)*

"Declaration
3 (1) It is hereby declared as the broadcasting policy for Canada that:
(a) the Canadian broadcasting system shall be effectively owned and controlled
by Canadians;
(b) the Canadian broadcasting system, operating primarily in the English and
French languages and comprising public, private and community elements,
makes use of radio frequencies that are public property and provides, through its
programming, a public service essential to the maintenance and enhancement of
national identity and cultural sovereignty;
(c) English and French language broadcasting, while sharing common aspects,
operate under different conditions and may have different requirements.
(d) the Canadian broadcasting system should:
(i) serve to safeguard, enrich and strengthen the cultural, political, social and economic fabric of Canada.
(ii) encourage the development of Canadian expression by providing a wide range
of programming that reflects Canadian attitudes, opinions, ideas, values and
artistic creativity, by displaying Canadian talent in entertainment programming
and by offering information and analysis concerning Canada and other countries
from a Canadian point of view.
(iii) through its programming and the employment opportunities arising out of
its operations, serve the needs and interests, and reflect the circumstances and
aspirations, of Canadian men, women and children, including equal rights, the

linguistic duality and multicultural and multiracial nature of Canadian society and the special place of aboriginal peoples within that society, and
(iv) be readily adaptable to scientific and technological change..."

(ii) *CBC Mandate (1991)*

The Broadcasting Act incorporates the CBC's Mandate in statute in s. 3 (1) sub-sections (l) and (m) as follows:

"3.1. (l) The Canadian Broadcasting Corporation, as the national public 'broad-caster, should provide radio and television services incorporating a wide range of programming that informs, enlightens and entertains;

(m) The programming provided by the Corporation should:
(i) be predominantly and distinctively Canadian;
(ii) reflect Canada and its regions to national and regional audiences, while serving the special needs of those regions;
(iii) actively contribute to the flow and exchange of cultural expression;
(iv) be in English and in French, reflecting the different needs and circum-stances of each official language community, including the particular needs and circumstances of English and French linguistic minorities;
(v) strive to be of equivalent quality in English and French;
(vi) contribute to shared national consciousness and identity;
(vii) be made available throughout Canada by the most appropriate and effi-cient means and as resources become available for the purpose, and
(viii) reflect the multicultural and multiracial nature of Canada..."

(d) Australia:

(i) *Broadcasting Services Act (1992):*

"s. 150: Objectives

(a) to promote the availability to audiences throughout Australia of a diverse range of radio and television services offering entertainment, education and information; and
(b) to provide a regulatory environment that will facilitate the development of a broadcasting industry in Australia that is efficient, competitive and responsive to audience needs; and

(c) to encourage diversity in control of the more influential broadcasting services and;

(d) to ensure that Australians have effective control of the more influential broadcasting services; and

(e) to promote the role of broadcasting services in developing and reflecting a sense of Australian identity, character and cultural diversity; and

(f) to promote the provision of high quality and innovative programming by providers of broadcasting services; and

(g) to encourage providers of commercial and community broadcasting services to be responsive to the need for a fair and accurate coverage of matters of public interest and for an appropriate coverage of matters of local significance; and

(h) to encourage providers of broadcasting services to respect community standards in the provision of program material; and

(i) to encourage the provision of means for addressing complaints about broadcasting services; and

(j) to ensure that providers of broadcasting services place a high priority on the protection of children from exposure to program material which may be harmful to them. (BSA, s 3)."

(ii) *Australian Broadcasting Corporation Act (1983):*

"s.6. Charter:

1. The functions of the Corporation are—

(a) to provide within Australia innovative comprehensive broadcasting services of a high standard as part of the Australian broadcasting system consisting of national, commercial and community sectors and, without limiting the generality of the foregoing, to provide—
(i) broadcasting programs that contribute to a sense of national identity and inform and entertain, and reflect the cultural diversity of, the Australian community;
(ii) broadcasting programs of an educational nature;
(b) to transmit to countries outside Australia broadcasting programs of news, current affairs, entertainment and cultural enrichment that will—
(i) encourage awareness of Australia and an international understanding of Australia attitudes on world affairs; and

(ii) enable Australian citizens living or travelling outside Australia to obtain information about Australian affairs and Australian attitudes on world affairs; and
(c) to encourage and promote the musical, dramatic and other performing arts in Australia.

2. In the provision by the Corporation of its broadcasting services within Australia—

(a) the Corporation shall take account of—

(i) the broadcasting services provided by the commercial and community sectors of the Australian broadcasting system;
(ii) the standards from time to time determined by the Australian Broadcasting Authority in respect of broadcasting services;
(iii) the responsibility of the Corporation as the provider of an independent national broadcasting service to provide a balance between broadcasting programs of wide appeal and specialised broadcasting programs;
(iv) the multicultural character of the Australian community; and
(v) in connection with the provision of broadcasting programs of an educational nature—the responsibilities of the States in relation to education; and

(b) the Corporation shall take all such measures, being measures consistent with the obligations of the Corporation under paragraph (a), as, in the opinion of the Board, will be conducive to the full development by the Corporation of suitable broadcasting programs."

(iii) *A recommended revised ABC Charter: The challenges of a better ABC (the Mansfield Report) (1997)*

"1. The principle function of the ABC is to broadcast, for all Australians, programs of information and entertainment for general reception within Australia.
2. In undertaking its principal function the ABC must:

(a) maintain an independent service for the broadcasting of comprehensive, accurate and impartial programs of news and current affairs regarding events in Australia and overseas; and

(b) broadcast programs which:

(i) contribute to public debate concerning issues and matters of importance to Australians;

(ii) respond to the needs of audiences for locally based news, information and entertainment;

(iii) reflect Australia's regional and cultural diversity;

(iv) meet the developmental and entertainment needs of Australian children and youth; and

(v) make use of Australia's creative resources.

3. In providing broadcasting services within Australia, the ABC must contribute towards the diversity of broadcasting services in Australia..."

(iv) *Special Broadcasting Services Act (1991/1998):*

"s. 6. Charter:

1. The principal function of the SBS is to provide multilingual and multicultural radio and television services that inform, educate and entertain all Australians, and, in doing so, reflect Australia's multicultural society.

2. The SBS, in performing its principal function, must:

(a) contribute to meeting the communications needs of Australia's multicultural society, including ethnic, Aboriginal and Torres Strait Islander communities; and

(b) increase awareness of the contribution of a diversity of cultures to the continuing development of Australian society; and

(c) promote understanding and acceptance of the cultural, linguistic and ethnic diversity of the Australian people; and

(d) contribute to the retention and continuing development of language and other cultural skills; and

(e) as far as practicable, inform, educate and entertain Australians in their preferred languages; and

(f) make use of Australia's diverse creative resources; and

(g) contribute to the overall diversity of Australian television and radio services, particularly taking into account the contribution of the Australian Broadcasting Corporation and the community broadcasting sector; and

(h) contribute to extending the range of Australian television and radio services, and reflect the changing nature of Australian society, by presenting many points of view and using innovative forms of expression.

3. The principal function of the SBS under subsection (1) and the duties imposed on the SBS under subsection (2) constitute the Charter of the SBS."

(e) Ireland

(i) *Irish constitution (1937)*

"Article 40: Personal rights:
6.
1. The State guarantees liberty for the exercise of the following rights, subject to public order and morality:
(i) The right of the citizens to express freely their convictions and opinions.
The education of public opinion being, however, a matter of such grave import to the common good, the State shall endeavour to ensure that organs of public opinion, such as the radio, the press, the cinema, while preserving their rightful liberty of expression, including criticism of Government policy, shall not be used to undermine public order or morality or the authority of the State..."

(ii) *Taoiseach (Prime Minister) Sean Lemass: Draft programme 'guidelines' for RTÉ-TV (1960).*
In March 1960 Sean Lemass proposed setting out Policy Directives of a very general character to be given to the board and the Director of Radio Éireann as follows:
"The directives I have in mind would not lay down very rigid rules but would convey the views of Government on how particular problems likely to arise should be dealt with, and would imply that the persistent ignoring of these views would probably involve corrective action by the Government."
The memo went on to outline eight areas of possible contention such as the image of Ireland. This was to be of a "vigorous, progressive nation seeking efficiency." The Irish image should avoid "stage-Irishisms and playboyisms."
The presentation of features and comments on events abroad involving the policies of other Governments was to be the subject of a policy directive. Other matters covered were sex, sport and religion. He was advised against sending them but instead to incorporate the main policy points in a speech to the Authority at its first meeting.

Lemass wrote to the Secretary, "I think it is only fair and proper that the members and Director…should be informed of the Government's views as to how certain difficult aspects of national policy in their broadcast aspects should be treated, particularly as it is certain that persistent departure from them will force the Government to take action either on its own initiative or under pressure from public opinion. On these matters it is not enough to have the last word, if we do not have the first also…"

A new draft was prepared and Lemass made some amendments to it. He was still concerned with the presentation and treatment of image, the language, rural matters and Northern Ireland.

His view about Irish on television was that "the aim must be to revive that language by promoting the love of it rather than pushing it down the public's neck." The Taoiseach was anxious that the reporting of social problems should be upbeat. "The objective presentation of existing problems can be a valuable stimulus, when it is associated with constructive comment and a hopeful outlook for the future. But if, on a plea devotion to realism, the people's faults and shortcoming are exaggerated, or given a disproportionate place in the picture, the effect may be a creation of a mood of discouragement and pessimism. So great a disservice to the national interest would be inexcusable." *(Source: RTÉ archives).*

(iii) *Broadcasting Authority (Amendment) Act (1976)*

In terms of s. 13, RTÉ must:
"be responsive to the interests and concerns of the whole community, be mindful of the need for understanding and peace within the whole island of Ireland, ensure that the programmes reflect the varied elements which make up the culture of the people of the whole island of Ireland, and have special regard for the elements which distinguish that culture and in particular for the Irish language;
uphold the democratic values enshrined in the Constitution, especially those relating to rightful liberty of expression, and
have regard to the need for the formation of public awareness and understanding of the values and traditions of countries other than the State, including in particular those of such countries which are members of the European Economic Community."

(f) New Zealand

(i) *NZ Bill of Rights Act (1990):*

"An Act—
(a) To affirm, protect, and promote human rights and fundamental freedoms in New Zealand; and
(b) To affirm New Zealand's commitment to the International Covenant on Civil and Political Rights...
s. 13: Democratic and Civil Rights...
Freedom of thought, conscience, and religion.
Everyone has the right to freedom of thought, conscience, religion, and belief, including the right to adopt and to hold opinions without interference.
s. 14: Freedom of Expression
Everyone has the right to freedom of expression, including the freedom to seek, receive and impart information and opinions of any kind in any form."

(ii) *State-owned Enterprises Act (1986: reprinted 1995):*

"s.1 Principal Objective to be successful business:
1. The principal objective of every State enterprise shall be to operate as a successful business and, to this end, to be—

(a) As profitable and efficient as comparable businesses that are not owned by the Crown...

s.7 Non-commercial activities—
Where the Crown wishes a State enterprise to provide goods or services to any persons, the Crown and the State enterprise shall enter into an agreement under which the State enterprise will provide the goods or services in returr. for the payment by the Crown of the whole or part of the price thereof."

(iii) *Broadcasting Act (1989: reprinted 1998):*

"s. 36 Functions of Commission—the functions of the Commission (note: which markets itself as New Zealand on Air) are—

(a) To reflect and develop New Zealand identity and culture by—

(i) Promoting programmes about New Zealand and New Zealand interests; and
(ii) Promoting Maori language and Maori culture; and

(b) To maintain and, where the Commission considers that it is appropriate, extend the coverage of television and sound radio broadcasting to New Zealand communities that would otherwise not receive a commercially viable signal; and
(c) To ensure that a range of broadcasts is available to provide for the interests of—

(i) Women; and
(ii) Children; and
(iii) Persons with disabilities; and
(iv) Minorities in the community including ethnic minorities; and

(d) To encourage the establishment and operation of archives of programmes that are likely to be of historical interest in New Zealand—

by making funds available, on such terms and conditions as the Commission thinks fit, for—

(e) Broadcasting; and
(f) The production of programmes to be broadcast; and
(g) The archiving of programmes;

s.37 Promotion of New Zealand content in programming—The Commission shall, in the exercise of its functions under section 36(a) of this Act,—(a) Consult from time to time with—

(i) Persons who have an interest in New Zealand broadcasting and the production of programmes in New Zealand; and
(ii) Representatives of consumer interests in relation to broadcasting; and
(iii) Representatives of Maori interests,—

being in each case persons or representatives who can, in the opinion of the Commission, assist in the development of the Commission's funding policies; and

(b) Promote, in its funding of the production of programmes, a sustained commitment by television and radio broadcasters to programming reflecting New Zealand identity and culture; and

(c) Ensure that, in its funding of the production of television programmes, reasonable provision is made to assist in the production of drama and documentary programmes; and

(d) Ensure that, in its funding of sound radio broadcasting, reasonable provision is made to assist in the production and broadcasting of drama programmes and in the broadcasting of New Zealand music."

(iv) *Radio New Zealand Act (1995):*

"s 7: Charter

(1) The functions of the public radio company shall be to provide innovative, comprehensive, and independent broadcasting services of a high standard and, without limiting the generality of the foregoing, to provide—

(a) Programmes which contribute towards intellectual, scientific, and cultural development, promote informed debate, and stimulate critical thought; and

(b) A range of New Zealand programmes, including information, special interest, and entertainment programmes, and programmes which reflect New Zealand's cultural diversity, including Maori language and culture; and

(c) Programmes which provide for varied interests within the community, including information, educational, special interest, and entertainment programmes; and

(d) Programmes which encourage and promote the musical, dramatic, and other performing arts, including programmes featuring New Zealand and international composers, performers, and artists; and

(e) A nation-wide service providing programming of the highest quality to as many New Zealanders as possible, thereby engendering a sense of citizenship and national identity; and

(f) Comprehensive, independent, impartial, and balanced national news services and current affairs, including items with a regional perspective; and

(g) Comprehensive, independent, impartial, and balanced international news services and current affairs; and
(h) Archiving of programmes which are likely to be of historical interest in New Zealand.

2. In providing broadcasting services, the public radio company shall take account of:-

(a) Recognised standards of excellence; and
(b) Its responsibility as the provider of an independent national broadcasting service to provide a balance between programmes of wide appeal and programmes of interest to minority audiences; and
(c) The broadcasting services provided by other broadcasters; and
(d) Surveys which shall be commissioned from time to time to establish whether the audiences for the services provided by the public radio company consider that the quality and quantity of these services is being maintained.

3. Subsections (1) and (2) of this section constitute the Charter of the public radio company.
4. The Charter shall be reviewed by the House of Representatives at five-yearly intervals."

(v) *Television New Zealand Act (2003)*

"Section 12. The following Charter shall apply to all those parts of TVNZ that contribute to its broadcast content. It shall be predominantly fulfilled through free-to-air broadcasting. In programming for particular audiences, TVNZ is to consider all relevant provisions of the Charter.

(a) TVNZ will—

(i) feature programming across all genres that informs, entertains and educates New Zealand audiences;
(ii) strive always to set and maintain the highest standards of programme quality and editorial integrity;
(iii) provide shared experiences that contribute to a sense of citizenship and national identity;
(iv) ensure in its programmes and programme planning the participation of Maori and the presence of a significant Maori voice;

(v) feature programming that serves the varied interests and informational needs and age groups within New Zealand society, including tastes and interests not generally catered for by other national television broadcasters;

(vi) maintain a balance between programmes of general appeal and programmes of interest to smaller audiences;

(vii) seek to extend the range of ideas and experiences available to New Zealanders;

(viii) play a leading role in New Zealand television by setting standards of programme quality and encouraging creative risk-taking and experiment;

(ix) play a leading role in New Zealand television by complying with free-to-air codes of broadcasting practise, in particular any code with provisions on violence;

(x) support and promote the talents and creative resources of New Zealanders and of the independent New Zealand film and television industry.

(b) In fulfilment of these objectives TVNZ will:

(i) provide independent, comprehensive, impartial, and in-depth coverage and analysis of news and current affairs in New Zealand and throughout the world and of the activities of public and private institutions;

(ii) feature programming that contributes towards intellectual, scientific and cultural development, promotes informed and many-sided debate and stimulates critical thought, thereby enhancing opportunities for citizens to participate in community, national and international life;

(iii) in its programming enable all New Zealanders to have access to material that promotes Maori language and culture;

(iv) feature programmes that reflect the regions to the nation as a whole;

(v) promote understanding of the diversity of cultures making up the New Zealand population;

(vi) feature New Zealand films, drama, comedy and documentary programmes; (vii) feature programmes about New Zealand's history and heritage, and natural environment;

(viii) feature programmes that serve the interests and informational needs of Maori audiences, including programmes promoting the Maori language and programmes addressing Maori history, culture and current issues;

(ix) include in programming intended for a mass audience material that deals with minority interests;

(x) feature New Zealand and international programmes that provide for the informational, entertainment and educational needs of children and young people and allow for the participation of children and young people;

(xi) maintain and observe a code of ethics that addresses the level and nature of advertising to which children are exposed;

(xii) feature programmes that encourage and support the arts, including programmes featuring New Zealand and international artists and arts companies;

(xiii) reflect the role that sporting and other leisure interests play in New Zealand life and culture and

(xiv) feature programming of an educational nature that support learning and the personal development of New Zealanders."

Printed in the United Kingdom
by Lightning Source UK Ltd.
99380UKS00001B/265-387